This anthology has been re-printed to celebrate the 21st anthology of the Alfred Fagon Award.

Alfred Fagon lived in Clarendon Jamaica, Nottingham, Bristol and London. He was a boxing champion, a welder, an actor, poet, and playwright. After his untimely death in 1986 his friends held a memorial evening at Tricycle Theatre to commemorate his life and work. The donations collected at the memorial formed the basis of the Alfred Fagon Award to recognise Black British playwrights from the Caribbean. The first award supported by Arts Council England and The Peggy Ramsay Foundation was presented to Roy Williams. The Peggy Ramsay Foundation continues to support the Award and the prize for Best New Play of the Year is now £6,000.

A bust of Alfred created by David G Mutasa was erected in St Paul's, Bristol. In September 2013 the Bristol Old Vic Studio dedicated an evening to him with a full rehearsed reading of his play 11 *Josephine House*. On 26th October 2006 the tenth anniversary of the Award was celebrated at The Royal Court Theatre in London. A reading of Alfred's play 11 *Josephine House* preceded the Award ceremony at which Lorna French was presented with the prize for her winning play *Safe House* by Diane Abbott MP.

Roland Rees chaired the Award from 1997-2009. In 2006 the founding patrons decided to appoint a new chair on three-year tenure. Subsequent chairs include playwright Winsome Pinnock (2010-2012) Anton Phillips (2013-2015) and current chair Brian Walters (2016-). The Alfred Fagon Award is now open to Black British playwrights of Caribbean or African descent resident in the UK

In 2014, the Award celebrated its 18th anniversary with the introduction of the Audience Award (voted for by the public in an online poll) and the occasional award for Outstanding Contribution to Writing.

In 2015, the Roland Rees Bursary (named in honour of the late Roland Rees) became part of the awards. The bursary is awarded to writers to enable them to devote more t

In 2016, the Alfred Fagon Award was granted charitable status and the Fagon family donated US$20,000 which will pay for the administration of the award over the next ten years.

Our gratitude also goes to our partner venues over the last 21 years The Royal Court, Tricycle Theatre and Royal National Theatre, and to the administrators of the prize Talawa Theatre Company, Tiata Fahodzi and Pauline Walker (PDW Productions).

And last, but not least, we salute our past winners, many of whom have gone on to forge successful careers in theatre with some even moving into television and film:

Roy Williams (1997 and joint winner in 2010), Shenagh Cameron (1998), Grant Buchanan-Marshall and Sheila White (joint winners in 1999), Adeshegun Ikoli (2000), Linda Brogan and Penny Saunders (joint winners in 2001), Trevor Williams (2002), Marcia Layne (2003), Michael Abbensetts (2004), Michael Bhim (2005), Lorna French (winner in 2006 and 2016), Allia V Oswald (2007), Paula B Stanic (2008), Oladipo Agboluaje (2009), Rachel De-lahay (joint winner 2010), Levi David Addai (2011), Michaela Coel (2012), Diana Nneka Atuona (2013), Charlene James (2014), Mustapha Matura (Outstanding Contribution to Writing 2014), Mark Norfolk (The Roland Rees Bursary 2015), Diana Nneka Atuona, Matilda Ibini and Mustapha Matura (Audience Award winners 2015), Theresa Ikoko (2015), Courttia Newland (The Roland Rees Bursary 2016), May Sumbwanyambe (Audience Award 2016), Mufaro Makubika (2017), Akpore Uzoh (Audience Award 2017), Beverly Andrews (The Roland Rees Bursary 2017).

We would like to thank The Peggy Ramsay Foundation for their continued support of the Alfred Fagon Award and Oberon Books for printing this special edition.

Yvonne Brewster OBE, Sheelagh Killeen Rees, James Hogan
Trustees, Alfred Fagon Award

Alfred Fagon

PLAYS

11 JOSEPHINE HOUSE

THE DEATH OF A BLACK MAN

LONELY COWBOY

OBERON BOOKS
LONDON

Lonely Cowboy first published in 1987 in an anthology called *Black Plays* (edited by Yvonne Brewster) by Methuen London Ltd.

First published in 1999 by Oberon Books Ltd
521 Caledonian Road, London N7 9RH
Tel: +44 (0) 20 7607 3637 / Fax: +44 (0) 20 7607 3629
e-mail: info@oberonbooks.com
www.oberonbooks.com

Reprinted in 2017

A catalogue record for this book is available from the British Library.

PB ISBN: 9781840021370

Cover photography by Andra Nelki

Printed and bound by Marston Book Services, Didcot, UK.

Visit www.oberonbooks.com to read more about all our books and to buy them. You will also find features, author interviews and news of any author events, and you can sign up for e-newsletters so that you're always first to hear about our new releases.

Contents

Contents

PREFACE

After Alfred Fagon died in 1986 a memorial evening was held for him at the Tricycle Theatre and a collection was made in his memory. We all felt we wanted to use the money to keep Alfred's name and work alive in some way. It took 12 years for this to bear fruit but with the help of the Arts Council of England and the Peggy Ramsay Foundation, the first Alfred Fagon Award was presented to Roy Williams in December 1997. Thanks to the continued support of the trustees of the Peggy Ramsay Foundation the Award is now ongoing and it has certainly achieved one of our aims in keeping Alfred's name in the public eye. Making his plays available to the public was a much more difficult task. James Hogan of Oberon Books has been an associate of mine for some years, and when we invited him to the presentation of the first Award it was his suggestion that Oberon Books should publish a collection of Alfred's plays to coincide with the presentation of the third award. Hence this volume; as Alfred's literary agent we would be delighted to hear from any company that would like to produce one of his plays.

I would like to thank all at Oberon Books, Roland Rees and John Cruickshank for their help in making this book possible.

Harriet Cruickshank
London 1999

INTRODUCTION

Roland Rees

I first met Alfred Fagon in a small sunny flat off Westbourne Grove in 1970. I was auditioning for Mustapha Matura's play, *Black Pieces,* produced by InterAction in their season of 'Black and White Power' plays at the ICA.

Alfred was quiet, even reserved, not a characteristic I was to associate with him during our friendship in subsequent years. He looked at the script in silence. Then he turned to me, 'You're not going to do this,' he said, 'Not going to put this on?' 'Of course.' 'But you can't have people talking like that on stage.' The black characters spoke in a real Caribbean language – it was written into the text – with all the speech patterns and rhythms so counter to English. As Alfred put it, the situation in the play was not unfamiliar to him living as he used to in Bristol, St Paul's. But the language he was being asked to speak for the audition amazed him. He had never before seen patois, an oral tradition, written down on paper. This was a clarifying moment for him and one which was to have far-reaching repercussions.

The other plays in the season were all from the black American experience. The success of *Black Pieces* lay in the fact that it was a home-grown product. There had been productions of plays by Errol John, Wole Soyinka and Barry Reckord in the fifties and sixties. But this production turned a corner, heralded a new wave of black writing for the seventies and made a profound impact on the audience. 'Black people were discovering a lot of things,' pointed out Matura. 'The history of their past and the way they had been brainwashed. That was coming out, so fast and everywhere.'

This conjunction of the *Zeitgeist* with his appearance in *Black Pieces* had an enormous influence on Alfred. It persuaded him that he could write plays with characters that could tell his stories, culled from his own experience, in a language natural to them. He was convinced that this would lead him to write plays entirely different in style and emotional content to Matura. He knew he had a very different voice. But the one lesson he had learnt along with the rest of the cast was, as one of them – Oscar James – said, they now knew they did not have to try to be English anymore. The conscious decision on Matura's part to have West Indians talking West Indian blew away all the cobwebs and loosened a generation of writers and actors – no one more so than Alfred Fagon himself.

Rehearsals were in a leaking, disused post office building. We had to clear the rubble to make a space to work. In other circumstances this would have been a real downer but such was the enthusiasm and sense of occasion that good feelings dominated all. During rehearsal I came to appreciate the distinct identity of the different islands. Most of the black cast were from Trinidad, Alfred from Jamaica. I remember there was much sending up of each other – giving 'fatigue' – and Alfred was the butt of most of this joshing. The Trinis felt they were cosmopolitan, city guys, and used to 'fatigue' Alfred about being a country boy from Clarendon in the heart of Jamaica, by imitating his gait as if he was taking large steps through long grass! It was all accomplished with a great deal of affection.

His parents kept a post office in Clarendon and there he was born 25 June 1937 into a large and close family of eight brothers and two sisters, leaving school at 13 and working with his father as a cultivator on their orange plantation.

The rest of his brothers and sisters made their careers in the States but Alfred came to the UK, first living in Nottingham where he worked for British Rail. In 1958 he joined the Royal Corps of Signals, becoming their middle-weight boxing champion – physical fitness continued to play a key role in his daily life. He left the army in 1962 to travel and sing calypso, eventually moving to Bristol where he trained and worked as a welder and here it was that he started acting on television for HTV. When we met he had moved to London and was staying in the flat of three English solicitors in Barnes. This combination of direct contrasts was essential Alfred. He could be demure, motionless and silent one minute, gargantuan, life-enhancing and loud the next, qualities that always permeated the characters in his plays as did the streak of poetic invention that interfused his own conversation.

Alfred's first produced play was *11 Josephine House*, presented by Foco Novo with InterAction in 1972 at the Almost Free Theatre in Rupert Street, off Shaftesbury Avenue. The cast I assembled reads very well today – Oscar James, Mona Hammond, Horace James, T-Bone Wilson, Ursula Mohan and Alfred himself. In hindsight, casting Alfred was not a wise move but at the time there seemed to be no other choice. Acting in your very first play is asking a lot. Knowing when to be in character or when to enter dramatist mode produced many tensions. Turning over the pages of the playscript I used at that time, I stop at one and notice 'cut' written across the whole page. I can still remember what anguish Alfred suffered over this and the way he had to listen to the cacophony of voices offering advice, and how he defended his bible of words until he gave in – in this case.

Oscar James recalls Alfred saying how proud he was of writing it in three days: ' "Lawd God, Oscar!" He told me how many words it had in it. He counted every single word. He was inspired by acting in *Black Pieces* and *As Time Goes By*' (Matura's next play which was commissioned by Michael White, premiered at the Edinburgh Festival followed by a short season at the Royal Court and in which I cast many of the *Black Pieces* company).

Alfred's *11 Josephine House* is a very different kettle of fish to Matura's plays. Although both reflect the early seventies, we are not at the cutting edge of black/white relations in the Grove and Portobello Road but in the front room of a Bristol household in St Paul's which acts like a cocoon for the characters to dream about and squabble over their real spiritual and geographical 'home' – Jamaica. Living under one roof are David, (the youngest), his Aunt Gloria and Uncle Harry, Castan (a distant cousin) and Brother George, deacon of the local pentecostal church but unrelated to the family. Oscar James again: 'It was about West Indians bringing their own culture and community here, into England, into the English culture. How do you keep that going here? There is unity in that life, whereas the whole English system was tearing them apart. It is about exile. The love and respect that religion placed on a community in alien circumstances and how it held together.'

The first brief scene betrays a beginner's inexperience, being a little too schematic in its effort to set up the characters and the plot – David announces he is off to London to sing in a nightclub accompanied by his white girlfriend, Julie. At first Gloria, Harry and Castan are aghast. They are losing Gloria's sister's son, for whom they are responsible, to God knows what in the big, evil city. But they relent, club together and send him off with some money.

The rest of the play takes off in a rumbustious mood. It contains an authenticity of emotional power and is peopled with richly drawn characters, who viscerally expose their inner life. The story is filled with religion, drink, love and hate at every turn. Comedy turns into violence, emotional turmoil into farce. Gloria is smitten in a 'religious' way with George; Castan is jealous of the outsider George's intentions; Harry and Castan get Gloria drunk; George enters; there is a fight; George puts Castan out of the house; a drunk Harry receives the Holy Ghost (for the night) and Gloria thinks she has sinned and lost her faith. Into the middle of this fracas step David and Julie back from London.

JULIE: I don't think I'll ever understand. One minute you're all killing yourselves, the next minute you're the greatest of friends!

DAVID: There is nothing to understand. They are just simple people who is hard outside but very soft inside. Above all they want to be friends with everybody and for others to love them.

Julie is not a migrant far from home in an alien world.

Alfred's next project was a play for television – *Shakespeare Country* directed by Philip Saville for BBC2 in 1973. As its title suggests, it is the story of a struggle to define black identity in a country dominated by a literary cultural icon.

After painting a picture of an older generation of migrants in *11 Josephine House*, Alfred set out to capture a younger generation in their twenties, living in the same district of Bristol, in *No Soldiers in St Paul's*, directed by himself at the Metro Club, off Westbourne Grove in 1974.

Alvin has returned from an all-night gambling session to be confronted by a very angry Mary. Once again he has lost all the money she earns in her factory day-job. Soon Byron, Dickie and Hazel arrive, spelling out their troubles. The form of the play is circular, taking off in poetic leaps and bounds like the effect of the ganja they smoke, allowing the characters to expand and tell their stories. Byron fastens onto a favourite topic, the Vice Squad and white people, then Dickie takes up the baton on the same refrain – who will be arrested next? Alvin follows suit on 'no work', 'no money' and other people's luck at gambling, until finally the litany returns full circle back to where it started.

Despite his troubles, Dickie reiterates: 'I'll say it again, I'm not leaving England.' Despite the terrible beatings Mary receives from Alvin – she shows the weals on her legs – she loves him and will not (whatever her threats) leave him. It is a circular world. 'I can't get a job,' says Alvin. 'I might as well keep beating the woman and send her out to work.'

As in *11 Josephine House,* the experience has turned the characters in upon themselves, forcing them to feed off each other emotionally. Truly they are trapped in their room and as Alvin says, St Paul's is the biggest prison in England. This prison world – like a Genet vision – could have been avoided by staying in Jamaica. But necessity rules. 'The hunger in Jamaica is worse than the hunger in England.'

The play runs a knife-edge between the rock-and-a-hard-place experience of life on the front line and moments of outright farce. The close sees police and sniffer dogs raiding number 57 down the road. Then it is the turn of the gambling-house next door, with Alvin and Byron fearfully commentating on the action as they lie flat on the floor and spy through the curtain. Finally heavy, fast steps are heard on the stairs. The men all dive under the bed, hidden by the mattress, whilst the women wait for the knock. A card is pushed under the door. It is BT offering a new phone connection. Disgusted at the men's cowardice, Hazel and Mary try to push them out. The police siren wails, dogs bark and in total panic the men rush out.

About this time Alfred was writing a very different play – *The Death of a Black Man* – produced at Hampstead Theatre in 1975, directed by myself, with Mona Hammond, Gregory Munro and Anton Phillips. Out of a Habitat-furnished Chelsea flat, 19-year-old Shakie runs his entrepreneurial empire, selling 'Scottish best peat water' to American tourists on Kings Road and ethnic chairs made in Yorkshire by African migrants on a pittance to wealthy 'beatniks'. Jackie, aged 30, bursts into his flat and life again after two years. Boarding-school educated, beautiful, claiming to be a social worker in Camden, and apparently rich and living with a retired Jewish schoolteacher in Eastbourne, Jackie has left Shakie's and her daughter Priscilla at home in Jamaica. Why she has arrived and from what destination is not clear.

In this play all is definitely not what it seems. We are offered a great deal of information but little certainty that any of it is true. Indeed the pitch of high tension at which the characters exist requires this fragile, chiaroscuroed reality – a world of chinese boxes revealing what? A deep urgent need to make it in a white man's world and to achieve this at the white man's expense.

We are a far remove from the front line in St Paul's. Here the front line is the Kings Road and from the suckers parading that street, Shakie hopes to become a millionaire. Jackie does not believe a word of it. Nor can she understand how, 'Me, a big 30-year-old woman allow a 15-year-old boy to screw me in the middle of England and give me a baby', and how in her ignorance she allowed herself to sue a minor for maintenance.

Stumpie, aged 21, the third element in this triangle, arrives. Returned from Germany (or is it Africa?) with a burning desire to record a family of pigmy drummers – 'I want to put African drums on television with African faces' – he wants Shakie to finance the deal. As Stumpie and Shakie rap on about the 'thieving' of black music by white musicians and producers, the dialogue becomes increasingly peppered with the language of black nationalism and a return to Africa and roots. Shakie thinks Stumpie's a 'puritan dreamer'. His experience of the music industry is how his father, a well-respected flute player, never attained a more prestigious gig than a pub and remained in poverty his whole life through – 'So leave black people music in Africa.'

The turning point of the play and its title refer to the 'Melody Maker' report of the death of Shakie's father, found destitute and syphilitic in a Manchester gutter. This incident, Alfred told me, was loosely based on the life of the wonderful Jamaican alto saxophonist Joe Harriot. Shakie remembers how his father was eulogised by the white press – 'the greatest black musician in England' – and his heart hardens against this waste and duplicity. He refuses to attend the funeral. He wants to be strong, to achieve something for his father and so becomes drawn towards the possibilities of Stumpie's project. It is his way of mourning – to raise the money and beat the white man at his own game. To achieve this, they revert to conventional roles. They want to overcome but have bound themselves to a path of defeat. So the tragedy is shaped.

They keep Jackie as a prisoner in the flat as their asset. They intend to 'sell' her to a rich white man for his winter cruise in the West Indies. Jackie says she will kill herself before they can do this – 'It's in your blood, murdering people for their money. I am not interested in black power politics.' Desperate to escape this role of the prostitute working for her pimp, she cuts her wrists in the bathroon and it is typical of Alfred that this revelation is kept for the final speech.

Like much of Alfred's writing the play unfolds like a dream. Stumpie says of himself: 'I am not a person. I am a character. Black people's character, that's me! I am good, bad and indifferent!'

Tecee (Gordon Case) and Bees (Stefan Kalipha) are pool hustlers in the 50-minute play *Four Hundred Pounds,* set in Finsbury Park during the late seventies. It captures the pitch moment in the break-up of a successful professional relationship. Tecee has refused to sink the final black ball with the white, potting instead the white and so losing the wager on the game – the title sum of money.

TECEE: Four hundred years all end in a day!

BEES: Are you saying the black ball represents black people in your head?

Produced as a double bill by myself for Foco Novo in 1982 with Howard Brenton's adaptation of Brecht's *Conversations in Exile* with the same cast, it toured the UK and played at the Royal Court.

Tecee and Bees are old friends from way back in Jamaica. There, working as mechanics, they dreamed of being a successful racing-car team. Now into their thirties and living in London, playing a good game of pool has become their earner. They set up their headquarters in a room rented from white squatters, decorate it and install a pool table. But Tecee has become disillusioned with this life, complaining to Bees that all he thinks about is money. 'Black people's life in England always seem to end up in places like this.' The spiritual side to him is not being nourished. Bees is a gambler, his interest is the action on the table and he believes he has witnessed a 'deliberate crime against him'. Tecee says, 'Jesus' hand reached out across the table and stop me from sinking the black ball'.

They nearly come to blows; a lot of money was at stake and an easy shot in place for Tecee. But Bees has to accept that something has changed for Tecee. He wants to return to studying at college.

TECEE: You know if I was a good swimmer I don't know what I would do – I mean now, right now water, water, swim, swim – I sure the wheel of fortune is still spinning and my heart used to beat faster than how it is beating now.

They divide the remaining cash but when Bees reveals that he placed £1,000 of their postal orders from their savings as a side bet on the final shot, Tecee erupts: 'Battle-stations, battle-stations to rass!' In typical Fagon fashion, a dramatic coup is left for the final moment. What starts as a serious struggle dissolves into hysterical laughter. A partnership has passed but a friendship remains.

Four Hundred Pounds is a study of the way the pressure of earning a living in London takes its toll, forced as the characters are to find work outside the conventional labour market. Tecee misses the days 'when we was young and drove a car on narrow roads in Jamaica'. He feels the experience of being in touch with 'home' is diminishing and he fears the loss. Bees has an explanation: it is 'the English ghost and the Jamaican Dobyadem dat fucking up your head!'

Whilst at the Royal Court Alfred and Howard Brenton held a reading of their poetry. It is a reminder of the other string to Alfred's bow and how his poetic instinct enhanced his plays with rich imagery. He was greatly influenced by his reading of the Bible, liberal quotations from it adorning his characters' speeches, and Milton was one of his favourite poets, he himself quoting sections learnt by heart. At his death he had completed a collection of poetry called *Waterwell.*

Alfred Fagon's last play was produced at the Tricycle Theatre in 1985, one year before fate brutally cut short his life. *Lonely Cowboy* was a new departure for Alfred. He deliberately chose to make all of his characters young – their early twenties – but, most significantly, English second-generation black. Here was Alfred re-fashioning himself, learning from the new sounds emerging from Brixton in the early eighties. This was a typical step for a man who passed through many phases and crossed so many barriers in his life.

One other feature of *Lonely Cowboy* is striking. None of his other plays are so infused with the atmosphere of place. In *Lonely Cowboy* home is here, home is that traditionally quintessential black location – Brixton. The place lies at the core of the play. It engenders a love/hate relationship in the characters. Flight, Gina, Thelma, Candy, Wally, Dalton, Stanley and Jack are young and in the moment of defining their world. It is the early eighties and the time of Afro and Rasta hairstyles, army fatigues, shoulder bags and bangles. They have hopes for life in Brixton. Yet the place keeps raising the question of identity. Is Stanley typical? He says, 'I was born in Brixton. Went to the East End to grow up and travel the world. And now I come back to Brixton to rest.'

Or is Candy's story more representative: 'Maybe my roots are not in Brixton,' as she thinks of flying the coop.

Flight and Gina open their new 'caf' – the 'Lonely Cowboy'. Freshly painted, with a mint kitchen and microwave, serving dumplings and salt-fish, juice, milk and punch, it is a new venture, intended as an oasis for shared hopes and dreams, from which 'music and back to Africa politics' are banned by Flight. It is also a haven against the front line and passing police sirens whose presence is only too evident right outside the door, the entrance through which the characters and the 'old habits' all too soon come crowding in.

'All roads in the world lead to Brixton's "Lonely Cowboy,"' announces Flight. No sooner is the 'closed' sign turned to 'open' than Flight complains of pressure – 'I over-excited', 'my stomach is unsettle', 'on the most important day of my life I can't seem to find my foot'. He wants to visit the front line, leaving Gina to manage the 'caf'. 'Shut your wicked mouth,' snorts Gina, 'are you selling ganja and running women on the front line?' 'No. I stop all that foolishness', insists Flight. But he is gone, 'on business'. To return two days and nights later with the excuse that he was trying to 'collect my money that I lend the man'.

Ganja is one of the main characters in the play. It invades their life from the outset. Gina is desperate at all costs to ban it from the 'caf', to protect their new life.

GINA: I can't stand that word. Ganja troubles upon troubles.
FLIGHT: I don't know sometime is only ganja money going around in Brixton.

This philosophic musing is accompanied by the sound of a police siren and a vehicle driving past.

Ganja figures again in the plot with the entrance of Stanley and his carton box, measuring, the stage directions tell us, 18 inches by 18 by 12. It seems a truck-load of the substance has fallen into his lap and he is keen to persuade Flight to become his partner in distribution: 'Look man, you've got a nice place. This is where we can make a good start of something big. Brother, my ship has come in. It is your lucky day.'

Flight is wary but Stanley persists: 'We could supply all the boys in Brixton with them stuff.' One thing leads to another and a fight starts. Wally tries to break it up but not before Stanley's carton is knocked to the ground, spilling its contents of 'weed' over the 'caf' floor. They shovel it back into the carton and moments later Wally finds an opportunity to run off with the booty, leaving his treasured bike behind.

So a comic interaction between Wally's bicycle (always cluttering the 'caf' much to Flight's annoyance), and Stanley's carton provides the opportunity for ganja to become the dramatic lever by which comedy turns to tragedy and loss. A *deus ex machina* which puts Stanley in jail and produces a terrifying finale.

But not before Wally warns Flight: 'Brother Flight this is your base. This is where you take off and land. If you mash it up you will have nowhere to land when you finish flying.'

In August of the following year, Alfred (returning from his customary daily jog) collapsed at the entrance to his flat in Silverburn House off the Camberwell New Road. On arrival at hospital he was declared dead and his body put in the morgue. The police searched his flat for evidence of next of kin. They interviewed neighbours. All commented how friendly he was, always smiling and laughing and asking after their welfare, but they only knew him – to use their description – as the 'coloured man who ran'.

The police said they found no indicators of friends, relatives or work colleagues. After five days the Southwark Coroner declared he had died of natural causes and the hospital administration took the decision, in the absence of anyone claiming the body, routinely to dispose of it. This meant that Alfred was cremated in a pauper's ceremony at the South London Crematorium with his ashes spread over a hedge, marked T91.

The first any friends heard of his death was two weeks later when his acting agent was rung by the BBC asking why he was not present at the first day of rehearsal for a new series he was cast in. There was an outcry in the press, an obituary in *The Times* and a memorial evening at the Tricycle Theatre where £1,000 was collected to commemorate his name in some way.

On entering his flat it was evident to anyone who took the slightest interest in its contents that there was every indication of friends and next of kin. The BBC script lay next to Alfred's bed and could have led to contact with the BBC. On his desk next to the Bible lay his union card, passport and letters. There was a diary with phone numbers. It was an act of gross negligence by the police not to have followed these leads. The young 'bobby' who searched his flat made assumptions – that this man was a loner, a black man who nobody would miss. Indeed the subsequent police enquiry found no grounds for pursuing the issue.

Thus his play *The Death of a Black Man* became a self-fulfilling prophesy as if he had written his own obituary. A famous jazzman dies in oblivion in a gutter and a writer is cremated without recognition by his relatives or friends.

But Alfred did not die in oblivion. In the first place, I am glad I was able to encourage James Hogan of Oberon Books to publish this volume. It will encourage further productions of his plays. So often in the UK black plays have a built-in obsolescence: they disappear after one production. The few exceptions are Tunde Ikoli's *Scrape Off the Black*, Michael Abbensetts' *Sweet Talk* and Mustapha Matura's *Playboy of the West Indies*, all of which have received more than one production. But the publication makes a second important contribution. It will strengthen the building of a strong black dramaturgical tradition, at the moment weak because the plays rarely get into print so there is no tangible proof of their existence.

But oblivion has been avoided in another way. A phoenix has arisen in the shape of an annual award – the Alfred Fagon Award – to encourage black writing in this country by writers from the Caribbean or with Caribbean antecedents. I feel sure that Alfred would naturally be both proud and at the same time doubled up with nervous laughter at this recognition.

Roland Rees
London 1999

11 JOSEPHINE HOUSE

Characters

CASTAN
distant cousin to David, Gloria and Harry.
Aged 42 – 44. 5ft 8ins or under

DAVID
nephew of Gloria and Harry. Aged 24

GLORIA
in love with George since childhood.
Aged 33 – 34

GEORGE
a friend of the whole family since childhood
days in Jamaica. Aged 39 – 40. 5ft 10ins or over

HARRY
thinks he'll get rich one day. Aged 37 – 38

JULIE
average English girl. Aged 22

11 Josephine House was first performed at The Almost Free Theatre as an InterAction production in 1972, with the following cast:

CASTAN, Alfred Fagon

DAVID, T-Bone Wilson

GLORIA, Mona Hammond

GEORGE, Oscar James

HARRY, Horace James

JULIE, Ursula Mohan

Director, Roland Rees

Bristol St Paul 1971.

The whole play takes place in one room. No change of set.

*Curtain – CASTAN is sitting on settee reading letter, mumbling.
GEORGE enters.*

GEORGE: Morning Castan, will you be coming to church this morning? Oh I see you get a letter from your daughter. How is she? Bless her soul. I have always have a place in my heart for your daughter.
(*GLORIA enters.*)

GLORIA: Morning Brother George, how are you this morning? Castan we were hoping and praying to the Lord for your safe return. Good news from your daughter? How is her husband?

HARRY: That boy should have never come to England. He sits in his room playing records and smoking drugs with white woman. Day and night. The police is going to raid the house.

GLORIA: I do not see how he could give up his mother for a white woman.

GEORGE: That is true Sister Gloria. I have given up all hopes for the boy. Where does he get his money from? God in heaven knows. What is he doing with those white women? I promised his mother, bless her heart, she's such a nice lady, that I would look after the boy, but I am afraid since he hit the foreman and disgraced the black people who work in the factories I have given up praying for him.

CASTAN: Jesus Christ, when will I see my daughter again? She's going to have a baby. I am going to the pub. Where is David?

GLORIA: In his room with his white woman.

GEORGE: Why don't you speak to the boy Brother Castan?

HARRY: Why don't you give up looking after the boy? He's going to disgrace you with the police.

CASTAN: Brother George you're a man of God so why don't you help him if you think he needs help?

GLORIA: May the Lord forgive you. How can you speak to Brother George like that?

GEORGE: No, no, Sister Gloria, the Lord work in a mysterious way. I too was a sinner once. Thank God I respect my father to this day.

CASTAN: Alright Brother George, I will speak to him.

HARRY: I am going to bust his rass cloth head one day.

GLORIA: Harry please remember Brother George is in here. The boy is causing us all to sin. Oh my God, the boy is so bad.

CASTAN: If he is wrong the Lord will punish him.

HARRY: I have to work hard for my money. I shall not lift a finger to save him.

CASTAN: Sometime I think all of you are worse than David.

GLORIA: Castan, it's you and David who send Mr James to the madhouse. You are both wicked and evil. You did not want to pay the rent.

CASTAN: Gloria since the day I know you you have always want Brother George.

HARRY: Since that boy come to England and come in this house there is no peace. I shall glad for the day when the police get him. I shall not lift a finger to save him.

CASTAN: You have never liked the boy, do you Harry?

GLORIA: Castan, you are evil man. Who lent you the money to pay for your daughter passage, and then you talk about Brother George.

HARRY: I hate the rass cloth boy.

GEORGE: Stop. There will be no hate in this house. Today is Sunday. It is a day of rest. Come along Sister Gloria. We will be late for church. Oh Lord have mercy I shall pray for all of you in this house. Some brothers and sisters will be coming down from Birmingham. Some of them will be coming back here for refreshment. Please do not disgrace me in front of these people. Castan, will you please tell David for me.

(*GLORIA and GEORGE exit.*)

HARRY: You can't trust black people at all.

CASTAN: That's right, Harry, and you are one of the people black people can't trust.

HARRY: You are a rass clath thief, Castan. You and your
dad used to thieve chickens when you was in Jamaica.

CASTAN: Look who is talking. You come from the country,
come to Kingston and work as yardboy.

HARRY: Ah, see, while you was pushing handcart all over
Kingston market.

CASTAN: Kiss my rass clath Harry Davies, I am going to
fuck you up right now.

HARRY: You can't do me nothing. I was better than you in
Jamaica and I am still better than you.

DAVID: (*Off.*) Will you shut up down there. I am trying to
write a letter.

CASTAN: I am going to kick your rass clath from here to
kingdom come.

HARRY: Go on, just try it.

(*DAVID enters, smartly dressed.*)

DAVID: What's the matter with the two big men like you?
(*CASTAN rushes up to HARRY and hits him. HARRY starts
screaming and rushes in the kitchen. DAVID pleads with
him. HARRY rushes in with a knife. DAVID leaves CASTAN
and starts talking to HARRY.*)

HARRY: I will hang for him rass clath. My dad stop hitting
me when I was 12. Murder in this house this Sunday,
I am going to kill him.

(*CASTAN rushes to the kitchen and comes back again with
the saucepan.*)

CASTAN: Let him come David. Just let me beat out him
blood clath.

DAVID: Is this what you come to England for to fight one
another?

(*Banging at the door. DAVID panics. He looks at them both
in a panic and goes to the door. HARRY and CASTAN stand
glaring at each other. DAVID returns.*)

Come on, pull yourselves together.

(*JULIE enters and stands behind DAVID looking in
amazement at HARRY and CASTAN who are still holding
the saucepan and the knife.*)

It's alright, Julie.

JULIE: Oh yes, I know. Hello.

DAVID: Alright. Will you please pack it in. You are not kids anymore. Julie, this is my uncle Harry and my cousin Castan. The deacon and my aunt is gone to church. They will be back later.

JULIE: Hello. Pleased to meet you. David talks a lot about you.

(*They both look at her but do not answer. They exit to the kitchen moaning at each other.*)

DAVID: Please sit down Julie. They are alright really.

JULIE: Thank you. Here you are, a present for you.

(*She gives him a bottle of rum.*)

DAVID: Thank you Julie. I need a drink. My family are a handful but they look after me. I don't think I could manage without them.

JULIE: You love them very much, don't you?

DAVID: Yes I do. I'll go and get some glasses.

(*JULIE stands up looking around the room. There are photos of the family all over the walls. She looks very pleased and smiles to herself. DAVID is heard offstage talking to CASTAN and HARRY. They come back in the room smiling at each other.*)

CASTAN: Hello Julie.

HARRY: Hello Julie.

JULIE: Oh I am so pleased to meet you. This is a very nice room. I like the colours.

DAVID: What time are we eating today?

CASTAN: I don't know David. Why didn't you ask your Aunt Gloria?

DAVID: Would you like to stay for dinner Julie?

JULIE: Oh yes, if your aunt doesn't mind.

HARRY: She would love to have you, and anyway you haven't met the deacon.

DAVID: I would like to say something to both of you. I am going to work in a nightclub as a singer. Julie is going to help me. She thinks I have got a good chance. Her brother works in television. He is playing with a big band.

CASTAN: Well, David, if there is anything we can do just ask. You are moving up into the world and that's very good.

HARRY: Yes, son, anything at all.

DAVID: What is the matter with you two? I am the one who is going to get rich. You see what I mean, Julie? Love at first sight. Come along Harry, pour us another drink.

CASTAN: I don't know how the deacon will take it, and your Aunt Gloria, she will be crying for a whole year.

DAVID: The deacon will pray for me like he always do

JULIE: I have never been in a Jamaican home before, but I was at school with a lot of West Indians. I was friends with most of them. We used to go dancing a lot together. They were much better dancers than me. I really love the way West Indians dance, always full of life and rhythm.

(*JULIE puts her arm around DAVID, they embrace and kiss.*)

HARRY: Castan, let we go and take a drink. Man I really feel thirsty.

(*HARRY and DAVID wink at each other, HARRY gives DAVID a broad smile.*)

CASTAN: Alright man, I understand. By the way, are you going to leave the house? You haven't said much, Julie.

JULIE: Oh no, but I am quite happy to listen to you.

(*CASTAN and HARRY exit.*)

DAVID: Well Julie, now that we are alone, not that it matters, what do you think of my family?

JULIE: What do you want me to say? Come on, you know they are marvellous.

DAVID: Thank you very much, Julie, you're a nice girl. I am glad you like my family. We are going to make a million between us. Where your mother and father live?

JULIE: Please don't ever ask me about my parents, not from me anyway. You are very strange sometimes David.

DAVID: Yes, I know, but it is because I love you.

JULIE: Who are you kidding? What about the others? Please none of that sentimental stuff. If you really love me don't talk about it, just prove it.

DAVID: What sort of girl do you think I take home to meet my family? You just wait until we get to London, I got lots of friends up there. You will see.

JULIE: Please, I am the one who's supposed to be helping
you. I know what you want, and I am not in the mood.
What do you take me for? I am not stupid, you know.
I saw all of you winking at each other.

DAVID: Christ, woman, you are really crazy. I don't want
anything. Let's go upstairs and play some jazz.

JULIE: Why upstairs? Why can't we listen to them down
here?

DAVID: Are you mad? The devil music in this sitting room
on a Sunday? You want Aunt Gloria and the deacon to
die right in front of your eyes? Please, I don't think I can
possibly explain. You'll just have to learn the hard way.

JULIE: What are you talking about, the hard way? Are you
a woman-beater?

DAVID: Please let's go upstairs and listen to some records
before the Lord's angels get back.

JULIE: I am only going to listen to records, nothing else.
I have only known you for two days. Alright, I am ready.

DAVID: That's the same thing I said in the first place.
Don't worry, you'll still be a virgin tomorrow.

(DAVID and JULIE exit, CASTAN and HARRY enter.)

CASTAN: Come on, let's sober up before George and
Gloria gets back.

HARRY: George, Gloria. Who the rass clath cares? Castan,
I work hard for my money and I love my boy very
much. He's doing very well for himself these days.
I shall visit him soon.

CASTAN: I cannot stand the weather of this country and
they don't even know how to enjoy themselves in this
country. I work 10 hours a day and the income tax man
take half my money. Harry, I tell you man, I can't even
save a penny.

HARRY: Come on, Castan, they are coming back. They
couldn't have saved many sinners today. Bring the
whisky and let's go upstairs. Come on, man, I don't want
to see them.

*(HARRY and CASTAN exit, GLORIA and GEORGE enter
very happy. GLORIA is fawning over GEORGE.)*

GLORIA: They all love you today, Brother George,
especially the brothers and sisters from Birmingham.
They were very pleased and happy. Brother George, they
love you. I have never seen or heard you preach like that
before, and you saved three sinners. You will have your
own church very soon. Oh Lord I am so happy. Brother
George, you're a great preacher.

GEORGE: Yes Sister Gloria, it was a good day for the
church and for all of us. Yes, Sister Gloria, we have come
a long way and we have got a long way to go. Sister
Gloria I had a dream last night and all day I could feel
Jesus and the Spirit working through me. I did not speak
for myself today. I have no control over my words. Do
you realise I was preaching for hours? I could not stop
the words. They were the words of God. I could feel the
goodness of the people in the church coming to me all
the time. The Spirit was speaking to me through the
Holy Ghost.

*(DAVID enters carrying a suitcase, followed by JULIE.
GLORIA looks in amazement.)*

GLORIA: David, what have we done? Why are you leaving?
Where are you going? And who is this girl? Brother
George will you please talk to the boy. Oh Lord, I have
worked so hard. I even say a special prayer for the boy
today.

JULIE: Oh, I am his friend. We are going to London.

GLORIA: *(Shouting.)* Castan, Harry, come on down here.
David is running away.

GEORGE: Come now David, my son, look what you are
doing to your aunt. She have given you everything.
She work so hard for you and the church. She will have a
nervous breakdown. Oh my boy, you will go to prison in
London. The whole family will be disgraced, and what
will your poor mother think? In Jamaica?
(CASTAN and HARRY enter.)
Stop and think. Look at your whole family around you.
We all love you David. Only this morning we were all
talking about you and what a fine young man you were
going to be.

GLORIA: Oh Castan, just look at my sister's son. Harry, please talk to him.

JULIE: What have we done wrong David? What is wrong? I think I am going crazy. I have never seen anything like it. What is wrong with them? We are not going to South Africa you know, we are only going to London.

DAVID: For God's sake Julie, not you. Pull yourself together. Didn't Uncle Harry and Cousin Castan tell you that I was going?

(*HARRY and CASTAN shrug their shoulders.*)

Look, will you please listen to me. I am not running away. (*JULIE puts her arm around DAVID.*)

GLORIA: Take your hands off him and keep away from my sister's son.

DAVID: Oh shut up, Aunt Gloria.

GEORGE: David, watch your mouth and your language in this house on this Sunday.

(*GLORIA puts her hands over her face and cries. HARRY and CASTAN exit towards the kitchen, stop, and take a drink from whisky bottle.*)

DAVID: Look, sir, Aunt Gloria have nothing to worry about. Julie have been very good to me.

GLORIA: Haven't we been good to you too? Haven't we work hard for you? My sister scrub floor in Jamaica to give you education and work day and night to feed you.

(*CASTAN and HARRY enter. HARRY has bottle behind back.*)

DAVID: Will you all please listen to me.

JULIE: Gloria, you have got it all wrong.

(*HARRY drops the bottle of whisky. CASTAN falls to his knees on the floor. GLORIA looks at JULIE in amazement. GEORGE looks in the opposite direction. DAVID puts his hand across his forehead.*)

DAVID: (*Shouting.*) For God's sake, shut up Julie.

(*JULIE very confused starts crying and rushes for the door. DAVID rushes after her and brings her back.*)

Now will you all just listen to me. As I was saying before, Julie is very good to me. She has been helping me. (*He turns to JULIE.*) You should have called her Aunt Gloria or Sister Gloria.

(*EVERYONE relaxes.*)

JULIE: But I didn't mean to upset anyone.

(*DAVID puts a finger over her mouth.*)

DAVID: I am going to London to work in a nightclub.

(*HARRY and CASTAN start singing.*)

GLORIA: God will punish you two devils for this. Oh God, they have been drinking and sinning all day while we were praying for their wicked souls in church.

GEORGE: Go on, David, with what you were saying.

DAVID: Thank you, sir. Julie has her car outside. She is going to drive me to London. Nothing is going to happen to me. Her brother is going to put me up and I am going to work with her brother. Believe me, I am only going away to better myself. Her brother work on television.

HARRY: My nephew.

CASTAN: You're a good boy, David.

GLORIA: Why didn't you say that in the first place before you try to give us all heart failure?

GEORGE: Well, David, have you got any money?

DAVID: I have got a little, sir, but I don't need much. I will be alright.

GEORGE: That's good. Alright, David, will you and your lady friend please wait in the kitchen.

(*DAVID and JULIE exit.*)

Now the boy is going away and there is nothing we can do about it. Perhaps he's a man. Only the Lord knows that, so we shall give him whatever we can afford and wish him health and happiness in Jesus name.

GLORIA: I will get my purse.

HARRY: I have got my wallet with me.

CASTAN: Yes, the boy can have anything I can afford.

GEORGE: Sister Gloria, will you bring me my collection box.

CASTAN: Do you think he will be alright, Brother George? After all, London is a big place. Oh God, my heart jump. I hope he'll be alright.

HARRY: It is a very sad day in the house. He is a good boy and he has always respect us. With all the bad ways the

boy might have got he is still very good and I think
he'll be alright in London. I am sure he understand
white people more than us.

(*GLORIA takes collection box from glass case and puts it on
the table.*)

GEORGE: Come now, let's say a prayer for the boy. The
Lord know more about him than we do. He will guide
him. That boy has known nothing but love in this house.
Let us just give him what we can afford and then we will
all kneel and pray for him.

GLORIA: Brother George, is the brothers and sisters from
Birmingham coming here for refreshment? That will be
very good. So if we all wait for a little while then we all
could kneel and pray for the poor child. I am still not
satisfied with him going off with a white woman.

CASTAN: Yes, Gloria, that is true, and we all feel the same
way as yourself.

GEORGE: No, Sister Gloria, the brothers and sisters from
Birmingham won't be joining us. Will you please fetch
David and his girlfriend.

(*GLORIA shouts to DAVID. DAVID and JULIE enter.
GLORIA looks at JULIE. JULIE looks at the photos on the
wall until she sees one of DAVID. GLORIA goes over to
JULIE and touches her. DAVID stands next to GEORGE.
CASTAN and HARRY start putting money on the table.
GLORIA starts crying. JULIE is very embarrassed and puts
her arm round GLORIA's shoulder. GLORIA embraces her.
GEORGE puts all the money in the collection box.*)

GLORIA: Please, my child, look after him. He is my sister
only son. His dad died when he was 10. I love him like
my own son.

GEORGE: Come, Sister Gloria, let us all kneel in prayer.
(*GEORGE shakes the money box and puts a few coins in.
GLORIA goes to her purse and empties it, putting all the
money into the collection box. GEORGE empties the money
box onto the table. They all start kneeling around the table.
JULIE looks at all of them in surprise. She walks over slowly
and joins them.*)

GEORGE: Oh Lord, help David to do the right things in life, and a special hand for the different road he may takes in life. Help us, Lord, never to forget him.

Curtain.

Some months later.

CASTAN and HARRY are sitting at the table in working clothes. GLORIA is heard singing in the kitchen.

CASTAN: I can't understand how we only got one letter from David. Do you think anything happen to him? I don't think that white girl he was with would get him into trouble. She seem a very nice person. Gloria seems to be taking it very well. She seems to occupy her time and mind these days with the church and her beloved Brother George.

HARRY: You know something, Castan, I love David like my own son who I work so hard for. He is doing well for himself these days. (*Pause.*) Castan, every time I go down the road and I see those lazy young boys wasting their time with those no-good white women and they are always in and out of prison, and you know what they have those white women doing, I can't help thinking about David. Still, I don't think he would do such a thing with his girl, and then again I don't know. Jesus have mercy on my soul. His mother would drop dead in Jamaica.

CASTAN: I don't think David would go to prison. He is very clever and he knows white people.

(*GEORGE enters singing to himself. He is carrying a Bible.*)

GEORGE: Hello, Castan, hello Harry, did you work hard today?

CASTAN: There is no easy work in England for black people. Black people have to work hard or thief. Brother George, do you know Miss Rachel's son from Montego Bay?

GEORGE: Yes I do. He is helping me with plans for my new church. Why did you ask? Is he in trouble?

CASTAN: No, but I work with him.

GEORGE: Oh, that's very good. I didn't know that. How do you get on with him? Such a nice young man. There will always be a place in my church for him, and he is such a good singer too. He is thinking of taking piano lessons from Brother Wilfred. He will also be a great preacher one day. Yes, Lord, he will always have a place in my church, and I know he's going to save a lot of sinners.

(*GLORIA enters from kitchen with plates of food.*)

Thank you very much, Sister Gloria.

CASTAN: It smells good, Sister Gloria.

HARRY: And I'll bet it will taste good too.

GLORIA: Stop teasing me, and thank you all very much.

(*GEORGE has more chicken on his plate than anyone else. HARRY and CASTAN look at each other. They all bow their heads.*)

GEORGE: Thank you for this food, Lord, and bless Sister Gloria for cooking it for us. I hope we shall not want, and Lord please feed those that are hungry on the street.

GLORIA: Amen.

HARRY: Castan, you were telling Brother George about Miss Rachel's son Clifford.

GLORIA: Well bless my soul, I didn't know that Brother Clifford was Rachel's son. Then he is Rufus' son. Oh my God, wonders never cease. Oh my God, I have been in England too long. I did not recognize him but what a fine Christian he is.

GEORGE: Yes, Sister Gloria.

(*GLORIA and GEORGE look into each other's eyes.*)

I have only learnt this from Castan tonight. You and I, Sister Gloria, can remember when Rufus did not have nothing to feed his children with, but Rachel stand by him and they work in the fields side by side just to get food for the children. I used to give Rachel words of encouragement. She was a proud woman and very good-looking too. Everybody respect her. Rufus used to drink and gamble, and although he support the devil's cause he still used to feed his children, thank God. And yes, Lord, today his son, Brother Clifford, is in England helping me with my church. I used to pray for them then and I am still praying for them now.

GLORIA: Yes, Brother George, and you are still praying for them and your prayers are helping us in this house. We do not have much, but we never go hungry. Thank you Jesus.

GEORGE: Thank you, Sister Gloria, you are very kind.
(*GEORGE nudges CASTAN. GLORIA tries to put her arm round GEORGE. She stops and looks at CASTAN and HARRY, and starts eating again.*)

HARRY: Castan, you were telling Brother George about Miss Rachel's son.

CASTAN: Yes, Brother George, as I was saying, we work together and he was telling me about the church and how the congregation was getting bigger every week and even white people are coming in to listen to you and everybody, including the white people, put a lot of money in the collection box. Brother George, I don't think you should keep such a large sum of money in the house.

GEORGE: Oh no, Castan, the money has been going into Barclays Bank every Monday.

GLORIA: Barclays Bank is a good bank. They have them all over Jamaica. When Phillip used to send me money for my passage to come to England I used to save it in Barclays Bank. And the little that I still save goes into Barclays Bank.

HARRY: Yes, Brother George, even down the bookie and in the pub they are all talking about you and the church and how everybody respects you and how rich the church is getting.

GEORGE: Thank you for telling me what the people is saying about me. You have given me much strength. The Lord work is never finished. Please excuse me I have to hurry. I am calling on some sisters and brothers tonight. Sister Mary, bless her, is very weak. I think the cold weather is too much for her. The doctors have given up all hope for her. All she is doing is calling for me day and night. I must go and see her tonight. I must also call on Sister Sally. Her son has broke into some white people's gas meter again and the police have got him in jail. She needs comforting. The boy must have had curse from his father's side of the family. Yes, Lord, I must hurry.

(*GLORIA starts clearing the table. GEORGE and GLORIA exit with the plates.*)

CASTAN: Harry, I heard you had a win at the bookie today man.

HARRY: Now who the rass clath would tell you a thing like that? But wait, black people can't mind their own business. Jesus Christ, I will kill one of them one day.

CASTAN: Don't shout, man. You know what Gloria is like about gambling and you know Brother George is still in the house.

HARRY: Castan, you are a rass clath fool. Gloria is my sister, but I can't help thinking about the way she is looking at her Brother George.

(*GLORIA is heard singing in the kitchen.*)

Just listen to her. Mark my word, the other one will be coming down the stairs singing as well. I am not sure if God will not strike them both down one day.

CASTAN: Harry, you are the worst black man in the world. I asked about the money you win on the horses and you are telling me about George and Gloria. Why are you so mean, Harry man. Whatever George and Gloria do, that is their business. They are responsible for their own sin, so mind your own business the way I mind my business, and nobody can say I do anything.

HARRY: But she's my sister, man, and suppose she get pregnant. Who is going to look after her baby?

CASTAN: What the rass clath are you talking about? I ask you how much money you win in the bookie shop and you telling me one set a rass clath in my ear. Man, give me one two pounds out the winnings.

(*GLORIA enters still singing.*)

GEORGE: (*Pokes head round door.*) Please do not wait up for me Sister Gloria.

GLORIA: Have a safe journey. I am sure they will be pleased to see you.

GEORGE: Thank you Sister Gloria.

GLORIA: That a glorious man. A sure saint for heaven if ever I see one. Castan, Harry, you should see him in church these days. Young and old fall flat at his feet. I am so proud and honoured to be in his church. Yes, I love the church.

HARRY: Gloria, me and Castan is very worried about you and your Brother George. Well, we don't think it is right.

CASTAN: That's right, Gloria. I for one is very dissatisfied. Indeed you seem to forget your family completely. I can't imagine what you got into your head.

GLORIA: That is the thanks I get from you. I wash and cook and scrub the house day and night. Only yesterday Sister Sarah was saying that I will die before the winter finish. Working my fingers to the bone for my family in this house, only the Lord knows how I manage, and you wicked sinners sit here and accuse me of carrying-ons with Brother George. You wicked and evil relations of mine shall punish in hell for this.

HARRY: That's exactly what we mean, Gloria. You are my sister and mother love us dearly. There was no favourite between us at home, but these days you seem to forget about David, our own flesh and blood. We only got one letter from him in over three months. I think one of us should go up to London. Maybe something have gone wrong. Suppose he's sick or in prison.

CASTAN: Yes, me and David was very close. He has got bad ways about him, but he was good. If any one of us was sick he would look after us. But suppose he is in hospital.

GLORIA: I cannot sleep night or day with worries for the child. If I was a man I wouldn't just sit here I would have gone to London to look for him. The minute I set eye on that girl I know she was no good for him. David was a good boy until he start mixing with no-good white girls.

They are living in sin all the time. I am ashamed to tell my sister what her only child is doing in England. It is not right in the eyes of God for him to run about with no-good woman.

HARRY: Yes, I get worried more every day. Maybe he is in need of help and money. Castan, we should go to London and look for David.

CASTAN: I was thinking Timothy is a good driver. He used to drive truck in Jamaica. We could give him some money and he could rent a car for us and drive us to London. Lord, I hope he is not sick or in prison.

GLORIA: Yes Brother George and myself will give what we can afford. Lord, I must get a bottle of tonic. My body feel run down with worries. My headache is getting worse and I think I have got a bad back.

HARRY: I have got one two pounds Castan, let us go down the road and take two water.

CASTAN: Yes, that's a good idea, but why not go and fetch it, man, and we'll all stay and have a drink.

HARRY: Alright. Good idea.

GLORIA: Will you get a bottle of tonic for me. I can't afford it, but the Lord know how I need it. I never seems to get any fresh air these days. I am working much too hard in the shoe factory these days. I will go and get my purse. (*She goes to kitchen.*)

HARRY: She will have a nervous breakdown one day. I hope that man of God doesn't let her down. Whatever happens she is still my sister. We have never done any harm to anyone. I have a few drinks now and then, but that's all the wrong I do. Only God knows how hard she works for that man of God and his church.

CASTAN: Alright, Harry, you said your piece. Go and get the drinks now. I will speak to her. But what can I say? Boy, this world is very hard.

GLORIA: Here you are, Harry, and please don't be long. I will have a glass before I go to bed tonight.

HARRY: I am only going next door, don't worry Sister, I know how much you need your tonic. (*He exits.*)

CASTAN: Well, Gloria, Harry, your brother, and myself were talking about you.

GLORIA: Please, Castan, the Lord in heaven knows that I haven't done anything to be ashamed. I work hard every day.

CASTAN: No Gloria, that is true. We are worried about your health and we trust you. We have always be a proud family. Why don't you take a few days off from work. You are sending yourself to the grave, and I think George should ask you to marry him. After all, you live under the same roof and people might start talking. You have never looked at another man, since that no-good man of yours walk out on you. Although he paid your fare to come to England he still no good.

GLORIA: No, Castan, I do not want charity and I want no man. Brother George is a man of God and I respect him for it, but I feel my duty belong to the church. Yes, I shall work to support myself. The work is hard but the money is good. When the new church come together I shall devote my whole life to the cause of the church. The Lord will give me strength to do that. When that no-good left me I will not mention his name in my mouth. I went to Jesus and I found peace in the church, and Brother George been very good to me. Bless his day, Jesus.

CASTAN: Gloria, you got a heart of gold man, but don't forget if there is anything or any time at all you feel like giving up work even for a few days or a couple of week, Harry and myself earn enough to keep you for a little while. Anyway, Gloria, let's all have a drink when Harry gets back.

GLORIA: Come on Castan, let's get David record player down here. I will listen to some of the gospel records Brother George got in his room but I will not drink. God knows what Brother George would think.
(*HARRY enters, CASTAN exits.*)

HARRY: Gloria, you are my sister, and there is something I must ask. As your brother I must ask you. I used to change your nappies. I am older than you. So tell me something. Has Brother George asked you to marry him? I know you are a Christian, but it is you who bring him to the house when James fell ill. In this case I can speak for Castan too. We have shown nothing but respect and he is truly one of the family. I must say I don't like people saying anything about my sister. We are flesh and blood. What is Castan doing?

GLORIA: Never mind about Castan. What is people saying about me?

HARRY: Well nobody is saying anything but you know what black people are like. You mark my word they will soon start talking.

GLORIA: I will leave them all to God. He will punish them the day they start talking about me. I have done nothing. I love my family. My headache is getting worse every day, but I still go to work and I want nothing from people. Brother George been good to me. He gives me encouragement and peace in my time of troubles. I shall mind my own business and still pray for my enemies. There is no hate or evil in me. I shall not marry Brother George or any man. I have just finished in telling Castan the same thing.

HARRY: But where is Castan?

GLORIA: Getting David record player.

HARRY: Don't tell me you are going to dance, Sister Gloria?

GLORIA: Oh Harry, you are evil and wicked. Mother should never have you.

(CASTAN enters.)

CASTAN: I did not know David was like that. He has got naked women hidden under the record player. But the boy bad you know Harry.

GLORIA: Oh Jesus Christ in heaven, naked women in this house.

HARRY: I am sure he done worse thing in his room. The boy piss will soon burn grass.

GLORIA: I know those white women was no good for him.

HARRY: Come on, let's have a drink.

CASTAN: Yes, just let me put a record on.

GLORIA: Harry, pour me a glass of my tonic. This headache of mine is getting worse every minute of the day. Oh Lord, work never finish. I must sew some buttons on Brother George shirt.

HARRY: Now look, Gloria man, you done enough for one day. Just put your foot up. I will give you a drink of my white rum. (*He goes to the glass cupboard.*)

GLORIA: You think I should?

HARRY: Of course you should. It's good for you. Nothing bad come from Jamaica. You will see, it will get rid of your headache.

(*Hot blue-beat music starts playing – they all start drinking.*)

GLORIA: Oh I feel good. Wish I could see my sister.

HARRY: Yes, she's a fine woman. I can remember the days when you and Mary used to creep out of the house at night to go dancing. You know, some time I think that mother did know about you and Mary going dancing before she died. I learn a lot from her. She was good to us Gloria, bless her grave.

(*CASTAN goes to record player, searches through records. GLORIA helps herself to the rum, HARRY is drinking a lot of whisky.*)

GLORIA: I used to enjoy myself with Mary when we were younger. That was before she had David. I can remember as if it was yesterday. Mother nearly beat her to death for expecting the baby. Yes Lord I wish I was back in Jamaica.

HARRY: Yes, I miss home very much. A man can't even enjoy themself in this country. You can't even get any good food to eat. Their ice-cream taste like shit house.

GLORIA: Harry, watch your tongue.

HARRY: Sorry, sister.

(*Calipsos are playing on record player.*)

CASTAN: Come on, Gloria, let's dance.

GLORIA: Oh Castan, I haven't danced for years. Lord have mercy. But I was a good dancer when I was younger.

(*They all start laughing and are mildly drunk. GLORIA is still drinking white rum.*)

But I have to leave those things to young girl these days.
(*CASTAN pulls her up.*)

Don't laugh at me, Castan Wright.

(*HARRY starts dancing by himself. GLORIA starts laughing.*)
Oh Castan, you're a bad man.

(*CASTAN and GLORIA start dancing very close to each other. HARRY goes over and changes the record. CASTAN and GLORIA continue holding each other closely and drinking. A Louis Jordan record comes on. Everybody starts dancing, feet moving fast, clapping and singing. GEORGE enters, kicks the record player. The music stops. All is silent.*)

GEORGE: Sin in the house of God! What sins are my eyes witnessing?

CASTAN: Where the rass cloth you get that from?

(*GLORIA takes her glass over to the bottle of tonic and fills it with tonic. She looks quite drunk.*)

GEORGE: Gloria, what are you doing? The devil take hold of your soul. You will burn in hell for this. Wicked sinners.

GLORIA: George, I have been drinking my tonic all evening, I swear to you.

(*GEORGE rushes over to HARRY.*)

GEORGE: Look what you have done to your sister. Sin, sin, sin in hell. Lord have mercy. She call me George. I will break every bone in your body.

(*GEORGE rushes back to GLORIA, slaps her face. GLORIA starts screaming and shouting about her headache and bad back.*)

CASTAN: I will kill your rass cloth for this, God or no God, I don't care.

(*CASTAN rushes over to GEORGE. GEORGE hits him in the belly.*)

HARRY: I will spend the rest of my life in prison for you. She's my sister.

(*CASTAN goes behind HARRY.*)

GEORGE: I will beat hell out of you in the name of God.

GLORIA: Police! Police! Murder!

(*HARRY hits GEORGE. CASTAN kicks GEORGE. GEORGE starts fighting both of them.*)

HARRY: Gloria, why did you bring a rass clath like this in the house?

GEORGE: Lord Jesus, I'm going to beat hell out of them.

CASTAN: Come on, Harry, let's hang him blood clath.
(*Loud bangs on the door.*)

GLORIA: Stop. Stop. Somebody's at the door. Oh God, police! They will take us to prison.

CASTAN: You're a lucky rass clath nigger, George. Me and Harry would sure kill your blood clath tonight. Boy, you really lucky.

GEORGE: You are all evil animals and curse will come on this house for the rest of your life.

CASTAN: If James should know what you are doing in his house, George, he would go madder in the madhouse.
(*GLORIA enters.*)

GLORIA: It's the funny miserable old woman next door. She said if we don't stop the noise she's going to call the police.

GEORGE: I shall not spend another night in this house. God-forsaken devils all over the place.

CASTAN: Just go upstairs and get your rass clath clothes, and get out before me and Harry kill your blood clath.

GEORGE: Hell is more than good for you wicked people. Sin, sin, sin. The 99 psalms will take care of you. God and myself will curse this house. Forgive me, Jesus. Curse your whole family. You evil men in the sight of God. I used to pray for blessing on this house. I would have given anything to relieve the people in this house, but the Lord have open my eyes. God never make mistake. You are all jealous of me. I have been washed in the Spirit, and the Holy Ghost is in me. All my sins are forgiven. You will all die before your time. You will never be able to support yourselves. You don't even know how to better yourself. Yes I shall leave this house. Yes Jesus, my brethren will never know about this. Their innocent hearts, bless them, Lord, they are the flocks of Jesus the son of Mary. May their innocent hearts remain in peace. Yes I leave this house. Yes Lord, and never to return.

GLORIA: Brother George, you know my headache is getting worse, but I am not complaining. Yes Lord, I am only carrying a part of the cross that Pontius Pilate caused Jesus to bear.

GEORGE: Yes, Sister Gloria, I am leaving and you will have to fast and pray for a long time, then with the Lord's help you may have the Holy Ghost again.

GLORIA: Oh Lord, no more. Yes no more Jesus. I cannot take anymore tonight. I shall go to bed although I know I will not sleep for a month. Brother George, there is no hate in my heart for you. I shall ask for forgiveness from you and God, and please remember me in your prayers. Goodnight. (*She exits.*)

CASTAN: Well kiss my rass cloth, Harry, you see what I mean man. We should kill him blood cloth. You see with your own eyes what he's doing to your sister, and she's my cousin. What are you waiting for, George. I have never met a man of God as wicked as you. Will you leave this house.

HARRY: George, I am going to speak my mind very frankly to you. I cannot hold grudge in my heart, not to someone that I used to love and respect, but me and Castan are two big men. You have no right to kick David record player. We have no other enjoyment or entertainment. Surely the Lord cannot hate us for a little dancing and merry-making. You have always been respected in this house since James went to the madhouse. I do nothing but go to work all day and some evening me and Castan go for a few drinks. Why should we bother to live if we can't do that?

CASTAN: George, it will be a long time before I forgive you. I do not wish to have enemy, especially with a man who claims he's from God, but in my heart I love everybody. Harry, Gloria and myself was very worried tonight, but we did not want to worry you with more troubles. We are not a church-going men, so we are having a few drinks tonight because we haven't heard from David in over three months.

46

GEORGE: Forgive me, Jesus, yes the devil have been testing our faith but we must not weaken. Yes the last months have been great trials for all of us. First David went away, then Sister Gloria start having headache, and although I'm about to take over my new church and I am a man of God, Lord forgive us all for tonight. Here we are, black men all the way from Jamaica fighting each other. I wonder if the cross I have to carry will give message from God. It is many years now since the Lord call me to the cross and I kneel at the altar and He send me out to save sinners. Yes Lord, that was a glorious day, the most perfect of my whole life. I can remember it as if it was today. It was many years ago. My poor father had ten shilling to feed us and he had not another penny in the world. Mother was very ill. He did not know where he was going to get the next penny from. Yes, I was a wicked sinner until then. I took the 10 shilling, forgive me Jesus; and went gambling. Jesus I remember when I lost the last sixpence and I look up to the heavens and I was not thinking about the beating my father was going to give me. But yes Lord, I was only thinking of my poor sick mother. Yes, hallelujah, and I could feel a change coming over me. Suddenly the tears start coming down my eyes and I was crying to the heavens, and I could feel as if a voice was saying to me 'Don't cry,' and suddenly flashes went across my face, lightening and thunder start striking in front of my eyes, and I was blinded, and then a voice said to me, it was so gentle and sweet (*He starts crying.*) and then the voice said to me, 'Do not be afraid, lamb of God, you are strong now, you have come to God,' and it was like the voice was far, far away and yet so very close, and the angel said to me, 'Your sins have been forgiven' and then the voice said, 'Your road will be heavy and long, but you must go out and preach the word of the Lord to the rich and the poor. Your place will be at God's side in heaven.' The voice said, 'Arise' and I arise. I went home to Mother. I went straight in her room. There was two people with her. She looked peaceful laying on her bed. And then she said,

'Son, I forgive you. Yes I know the Lord would call you one day. Yes only last night I had a dream and I know then. Son, the road will be hard, there will be lots of trials. May the Lord bless you, my son.' She close her eyes. She never open them again. I left the house that day with the guardian angel. That guardian angel is still with me, and now I shall pray very hard tonight. I am sorry I hit you, Brother Castan. Harry, please let us be friends again.

(*HARRY starts crying. CASTAN hangs his head in shame.*)

CASTAN: Please forgive us, Brother George, I did not know.

HARRY: Yes Brother George, we could be nothing else to you but good friends. Yes Brother George, do not blame yourself for what happen tonight. The Lord work in a mysterious way. I might use bad words and puts a few bets in the bookie now and then, but I have always love God and I have always been a God-fearing man. Yes I have seen in this house the happiness that God put in your precious soul.

CASTAN: I am glad you said that Harry. It is good to speak the truth about a God-fearing man, and you have proved beyond all doubt Brother George that you are one of Jesus' disciples. Please do not blame yourself when you go tonight. You was only trying to save us.

GEORGE: Yes, thank you very much. You must remember none of you is beyond saving. God is ready to help you day or night. Yes my friends, you two will take the word of God to the people one day. I also was a sinner once and I know how strong the devil is. Thank you Jesus for saving a place in heaven for me. Yes my place will be there when I die.

HARRY: Brother George, I am not getting any younger. My son is doing well for himself. When I heard from him last year. I have a good job and I have a little money save. I know I'll never go hungry again, and the Lord always provide a roof over my head. Yes God has been good to me. Many a time Jesus come knocking at my heart and I turned him away. I cannot resist the calling of God much longer.

GEORGE: Well, Brother Harry, please do not stop yourself from serving God if He's calling you. I know if He's calling you He have a special mission for you. Tomorrow may be too late. Come to Jesus and God tonight. I can feel They need you.

CASTAN: Listen, Harry man, when God call you Brother George won't be there. Please remember the man is going out of this house, so listen to me. You are wasting your rass cloth time. If you ask me, the man is a joke, Harry man. He said so himself. So, Harry man, don't hold the man up, let him go to his flocks.

GEORGE: Yes, the devil is working from all side tonight, but my God and your God, Harry, is stronger than the devil. Brother Harry, give up drink, give up gambling, do not look at the next man wife, think of life after death and everlasting glory and peace with God. Please do not let the devil burn your soul in hell. I am here from God to make the devil a loser.

HARRY: Yes Brother George, the dreams I have been having at nights makes me believe there is another life for me.

CASTAN: I will tell you what, Harry. The next life you will have is that you'll have to go to work in the morning and dig rass cloth trench on the building site, or else hungry, bust your rass cloth. What's wrong with you, Harry man?

GEORGE: Think of the dreams you have been having. Brother Harry, Jesus die to save your sin and mine, but oh no, not that evil man Castan you call friend. Jesus will wash you, Brother Harry, and your soul shall be whiter than snow.

CASTAN: What the rass cloth are you talking about? Soul whiter than snow? Trying to turn black man white. Well kiss my rass cloth. The white people put black people in slavery and now this man of God wants you white before you can get to heaven. I tell you, Harry man, I know this rass cloth was no good.

GEORGE: Brother Harry, this man is mocking God, but God let me stay here for a reason, so don't turn Jesus away. That is why I'm here, to help you along with Jesus.

HARRY: Yes Brother George, I know. These dreams I kept
getting and I also kept getting blackouts. Sometime
I just go into a trance at work and I am a healthy man.
I have always feed my body well. I have never been to a
doctor in my life.

CASTAN: Then it's time you go and see the doctor. You're
a sick man, Harry. Yes man, you really sick. All this man
of God want is your sister and the blood clath is getting
richer. Every day out of the poor black people who we
call sisters and brothers. George, you got your church
and a whole lot of fool black people following you. For
God sake, man, leave poor Harry out of it. He has done
no harm in his life. We grew up together. He also love
his sister. Oh God, he work hard in Jamaica to save his
passage to come to England. He's still working rass clath
hard on the building site for the little money he got
saved, and now you want the whole rass clath lot for
yourself. Come on, Harry, we should kill him blood
clath early on tonight, but it is not too late. Let's do it
now. The good God in heaven will forgive us.

HARRY: What are you saying, Castan man?

CASTAN: Alright, Harry, maybe we shouldn't kill him, but
let's throw the blood clath out of the house. Harry, man,
I could just chop up him blood clath face. Come on,
Harry, we can do it.

GEORGE: Stop you sinning, nigger. Curse your mother
father and children, you black-hearted devil.

CASTAN: George, you are the sinning black-hearted nigger
in this house, and you are going out of this house. You is
the one who is going to burn in hell. Do you think God
is a fool. He would never let a punk like you inside his
heaven.

HARRY: Oh Lord have mercy. Yes I want to go to heaven
when I die.

GEORGE: Yes Brother Harry, if Jesus is calling you answer
Him. Yes, God is telling me to help you. The Holy
Ghost is coming on. Yes, Lord, you work in a mysterious
way. The devil is in this house. Jesus is giving me

strength. The power is coming on. Yes, Jesus, I will put the devil out of this house tonight. The Holy Ghost, the power of God, the soul is pure. Reach out. God is stronger than the devil. Jesus is ready to help you, Brother Harry. Your place is safe in heaven. Do not weaken. The power and the Holy Ghost of God should be coming on in you now. Yes, Jesus tell me so. I shall put this evil Castan out of this house tonight. Just sit there, Brother Harry, and take in the Lord power that He is giving to you. Money cannot get you into heaven, so Castan leave this house now or I will put you out myself.

CASTAN: You must be rass cloth joking. A you a go out tonight.

GEORGE: The Lord know I don't want to do this, but the work of God must be done.

(*JULIE enters. Nobody notices. GEORGE grabs CASTAN by the collar.*)

CASTAN: Come on, Harry, help me. Julie, Julie.

(*GEORGE puts CASTAN out.*)

HARRY: Hallelujah. I can see a vision. Yes Lord, I am coming. Amen Lord, forgive me Jesus. Yes I feel free. Oh Lord let the fire fall on me. (*Singing.*) 'Fire, fire fall on me.' (*Speaks.*) Yes Lord, I have sinned and turned back from the road to heaven so many times.

GEORGE: Yes, let the Lord help you. Confess all your sins, Brother Harry. Tell Jesus everything.

(*GEORGE starts singing and clapping. HARRY falls in front of him.*)

Be strong, Brother Harry.

(*HARRY tries to climb up on GEORGE – GEORGE helps him up. HARRY begins to get the Spirit and starts jumping. GEORGE tries to control him. HARRY starts running round in circles, GEORGE follows him everywhere. JULIE runs out of the room shouting.*)

JULIE: Gloria, Gloria, anybody, they are going mad down here. Somebody please come quickly.

(*Toilet heard flushing. GLORIA rushes in.*)

GLORIA: Amen. Yes, I know Brother George would save my only brother.

JULIE: Shall I call the ambulance? Come on, Gloria, do something. What is it? What's happening? What are they doing? What's got into them?

GLORIA: Sanctify my soul. My child, it is the Spirit of the Lord that is working through them. Yes my dear, you are witnessing how the Holy Ghost of the Lord work.
(*GEORGE supports HARRY, singing. HARRY is mumbling about the Holy Ghost. Both exit.*)

JULIE: Is this some sort of a private ceremony? I am sorry I walked in like this, but David gave me his keys and I thought everybody was in bed.

GLORIA: Oh no, nothing like that. Harry is a Christian now. Oh Lord forgive me. How is my sister's son? But where is he?

JULIE: He'll be along very soon. He stopped off down the road to see some friends.

GLORIA: I suppose he has gone to the gambling house to buy drugs. Oh my sister boy is so bad, and please Julie don't worry about calling me Sister Gloria. I have changed.

JULIE: I didn't, but I still don't understand.

GLORIA: Well, I am afraid the flesh is too weak. I turn to drink tonight and I am a sinner again, but Harry is much stronger than myself. He will make a better Christian than me.

JULIE: I still don't understand, but every one of you believes in God. David said so. But you're all Christians, all of you go to church that's enough isn't it? God doesn't want more than that.

GLORIA: Please my child, the Lord will punish you for saying such things. Oh Lord, my headache is getting worse, and I am losing faith. Yes, I'm too weak, but if the Lord want me to serve his purpose in the future I shall gladly go to him.
(*DAVID enters.*)

DAVID: Hello, Aunt Gloria, you are up late.

GLORIA: But David, how well you look. Your mother would be proud of you if only she could see the fine boy you turn into.

DAVID: Thank you, Aunt Gloria. But where is Castan and Uncle Harry? Are they in bed? But Aunt Gloria, you should be in bed.

GLORIA: I don't know where Castan is, but David you would be proud of your Uncle Harry if you did see him tonight. I have never seen anyone get the Spirit and the Holy Ghost more than your Uncle. He is a Christian now. It happen tonight right here in this house. He receive the Holy Ghost. He will make a better Christian than myself.

JULIE: David, I was dumbfounded. I came in and I could not believe my eyes.

DAVID: Yes, I know what you mean.

GLORIA: I will have to say goodnight. My headache is getting worse. I don't think I can go to work in the morning.

DAVID: I am sorry you're not feeling well. Alright, you go to bed. Have you been to see the doctor?

GLORIA: No, a doctor is no good to me.

DAVID: Alright, I'll take you to the doctor tomorrow.

GLORIA: I don't know about that. But I hope you realize, David, that it is the Lord punishment for not putting enough faith in him. Goodnight.

DAVID: Okay. Aunt Gloria. You just go to bed. I will call you in the morning.

(*GLORIA exits.*)

JULIE: They are killing themselves for no reason whatsoever. I have never seen or heard anything like it. How come you are so different?

DAVID: What do you mean, I am different? Believe me, I am no different except they are more honest than myself. Oh, I know, it is very hard to explain, but while you are staying here you will see how simple and easy it is to understand, and how much they understand each other.

(*CASTAN enters with a big stick in his hand.*)

CASTAN: Where is the rass clath? He throw me out my family house. It's no use hiding, George. Come and

throw me out now. David, all I want to do is hit him
one rass clath time. He will never get up.

JULIE: I see what you mean, David. I think I am going to
be sick.

DAVID: Castan, what is the matter with you? Who hit you?

CASTAN: Nothing is wrong with me. It's rass clath George.
I am going to beat him to the ground.

DAVID: Who are you going to beat to the ground? The
deacon? But what has been happening here since I went
to London? I am getting very confused. Aunt Gloria just
tell me that Uncle Harry receive the Holy Ghost from
the deacon tonight, and now you are telling me that he
beat you up and throw you out. What a bloody welcome-
home present.

CASTAN: Don't blame me because he couldn't convert me.
He must a think I am a fool. He give Gloria headache.
Now he reckon he save Harry. More money for his
church. The blood clath hate me because him can't get
none of my money for his church and his pocket, the
lazy pussy clath.

JULIE: I can't understand a word he's saying.

DAVID: Julie, please do me a favour. Go to bed.

JULIE: You must be joking. And allow them to chop me up
in the middle of the night?

DAVID: Just shut up for a minute. Castan, where is the
deacon and Harry? No, sorry, I forget. Now Castan, you
just have to leave everything until tomorrow.

CASTAN: I am sorry Julie the things you see tonight, but
that man push me just too far. I am sure his mother curse
the day when he was born. No wonder his dad never
have anything to do with him.

JULIE: Why don't you take it easy? You are not fair to
yourselves.

DAVID: Castan, have you all been drinking tonight? Yes,
now I know what happen tonight. Come to think of it,
I could smell drink on Aunt Gloria too.

CASTAN: David, you are too young to understand.

DAVID: What do you mean, I'm too young? I am 24, so
what are you talking about? I know plenty more than

what you think I know. Look, Castan, why don't you go to bed and leave everything until tomorrow?

JULIE: Please, why don't you have some black coffee and sober up?

CASTAN: I don't drink coffee. All I want is to keep that man away from Gloria. I think I'll go and walk the streets. (*He exits.*)

JULIE: Stop him, David. He will surely get himself into trouble if he goes out of here tonight.

DAVID: You must be joking. He's only going to see his woman, I will bet you anything you like. All what the fight is all about is over Aunt Gloria.

JULIE: As soon as I think I'm beginning to understand I am back to square one. It is really very confusing.

DAVID: No, my dear, it is not. You just give it a few days and then you will understand the whole thing.

JULIE: I hope so, or I will go mad. Sorry, David, please forgive me. You know I love you. I am only worried about you.

(*GEORGE enters singing.*)

GEORGE: David, there is peace in the Valley of the Lord. Oh David, why didn't you let us know you was coming. This is very good. And how is your lady friend?

JULIE: Oh very well, thank you.

DAVID: Well I am very glad to be home, Deacon, and I must say you look very well. I am sorry Aunt Gloria isn't feeling her old self. I wonder if she's working too hard, eh Deacon?

JULIE: David is going to take her to the doctor's in the morning. She seems very upset.

GEORGE: Yes, the Lord does work in a mysterious way. I wish she hadn't sinned tonight. The devil bring disgrace to this house tonight.

JULIE: I don't understand. We only came here because David was so unhappy in London. The devil is not in me. I can't see how we bring disgrace on the house. I love David very much, but he puts his family far above me. He has got nothing but love for all of you. I am

very sorry we let you down, or maybe you think that
I am the devil. Well, I go to church sometimes and
I know all about God.

DAVID: Julie, listen.

JULIE: Oh shut up. It's about time somebody spoke the
truth. I don't care how much you lot have suffered.
The god in Jamaica is no different from the god in
England. You're all mad, and you're all killing each
other for no reason at all. Where is the love and soul that
you lot are supposed to have? I see nothing but fighting
and headaches and a lot of boring bloody people. Now
I know God wants all the blacks to suffer.

DAVID: Julie, what the hell are you talking about? Have
you gone mad? The deacon wasn't talking about us.
He is glad to have us home. They all love you Julie.
Please, please, just calm down.

JULIE: Oh David, what have I done? Please let us go back
to London.

DAVID: Don't you trust me Julie? What is the matter
with you?

JULIE: I am sorry, I don't know what came over me.

GEORGE: There is nothing to be sorry about, my child.
It is the work of the devil, or maybe the Lord is testing
our faith. I can see you are a person who speak from the
heart. God will also come to you one day. I can see that
Jesus want you to come to Him through me. If it is
tonight, let she see the light Lord. I shall pray for you,
my child. I shall pray like I never pray before. I shall
also pray for happiness for you and David to have a
good life in this wicked world.

JULIE: But please pray for yourself too. Don't give all your
love to other people. Save some for yourself. A person
can so easily misunderstand you. You spend all your
time worrying about other peoples problems, you can't
save the whole world. Some people have to go to hell.
Everybody will never get to heaven. I am sure God
wants you to think about yourself as well.

DAVID: Please Julie.

GEORGE: No, no my son, let she speak her mind.

DAVID: But Deacon, she doesn't understand nothing about you.

GEORGE: Then, my son, it is time she know all about me. A man of God have nothing to hide. Please go on, Julie. Don't be afraid.

JULIE: Oh I'm not afraid, but I have always seen myself as a good person, and I believe there is a God. I have never dreamt that my soul would burn in hell.

DAVID: I haven't heard the Deacon said your soul would burn in hell.

JULIE: I did not mean it like that. David, why don't you grow up?

DAVID: Who the rass clath are you talking to? I better beat out your rass clath. You think I am your boy? Never make that mistake again, calling me little boy. I'm a big man, you hear?

JULIE: I did not call you a little boy.

DAVID: Well what do you mean I should grow up?

JULIE: Is that what's bothering you? Oh, you are so stupid sometimes.

DAVID: Julie, I better kill you rass clath. I am not stupid. You are the one making a blood clath fool of yourself.

GEORGE: Good God, David, stop. I am ashamed, shock and very surprise. What will your aunt think if she hear you using the devil's language like that?

DAVID: I am sorry Deacon. Yes it is true, I should not talk like that in front of you. I lost my head.

GEORGE: I think you have lost more than your head. The devil might take your soul to eternity. Come David, my son, what got into you? I would like very much to listen to what Julie have to say. Please go on with what you were saying.

DAVID: Alright, Julie.

JULIE: Well, I don't know if I should really carry on. I don't want to upset anyone.

GEORGE: But I really would like to hear more of what you were saying.

JULIE: I am sorry if I upset you, David. I hope I don't do it again.

DAVID: Alright, Julie, but just watch your mouth.

GEORGE: Please go on, my child. Don't be afraid. This is a good house.

JULIE: Well, I would like to ask you a few questions. I am honestly trying to understand, but I can't help my feelings. I have got to speak the truth.

GEORGE: Bless you, my child, please go on.

JULIE: Well, I have always seen myself as a good person. I don't go to church every Sunday, but I have always believed I would go to heaven when I died, but the standard that you set is much too high for me. Don't think I am rude, but what exactly do you want from God and the people who follow you?

GEORGE: No, my child, I want nothing from anyone. Since that day I rob my father and my mother died the same day I do nothing but help people to get rid of their sins and put God in their hearts. I have been tempted many of time. Tonight I have to put out Castan out of this house. Yes, tonight I have save Harry soul. The day of judgement is very near and I do not want people soul to burn in hell. I want people to serve God, I want everyone to love each other. Yes Lord, I take the Bible with me everywhere I go. I shall go on preaching the word of God. Yes, I want people to fill my church, and I will fill their soul with happiness. We never stop fighting each other in this wicked world, but in heaven there is only peace. I want peace when I die, but I have to preach the word of God right here in this wicked world. I want to bring happiness to the poor, sick and hungry. Yes, my soul is filled with joy when I see all the happiness in the people who fill my church every Sunday. Yes, and they love God, and I love them for it. I want nothing for myself. I have got all I need, my Bible. Thank you Jesus.

JULIE: But that's not what I mean.

DAVID: For God sake Julie, please I will tell you what he want.

GEORGE: Please David, I can understand your concern. Let not be sad. It is a night of rejoicing. Your Uncle Harry soul is safe in heaven and your first night in the house. Let us thank Jesus for bringing us together again.

DAVID: Alright Deacon, you are right. Yes it is good to be home. I am glad you save Uncle Harry.

GEORGE: Yes, this is a good house. Just think your Uncle Harry will have nothing more to do with 'women', 'drinking' or gambling.

JULIE: That's very good. Then he will be able to save all his money.

GEORGE: Money cannot get anybody into heaven. Every man should cast their bread upon the water. Jesus take three small loaf and feed a multitude of people.

DAVID: That is very true deacon, because the Bible said so.

JULIE: David, you will be joining the deacon soon in his pulpit.

GECRGE: That will be a glorious day. Yes the church need young people to take the word of God to the nation.

DAVID: I think I better go on see Uncle Harry and let him know I am home.

GEORGE: No David, he is deep in prayer and the spirit is still with him. I am the only one who can speak to him tonight.

DAVID: That alright. I will see him in the morning.

GEORGE: Yes, when the roll is call up in heaven Brother Harry name shall be there written in golden letters. He shall be drinking milk and honey for ever and ever. The money that he promise me for my church I shall use it to put his name on one of the corner stones among the names of the other saints. The only thing that is evil in this house, I am ashame to say it, is your cousin Castan, the man is full of sin and blasphemy.

DAVID: Yes, I understand.

GEORGE: I shall go and join your uncle. I will tell him the good news that you are home with your girlfriend.

DAVID: Deacon, please see that he rest well.

GEORGE: Thank you both very much for being so helpful. The Lord will bless you both. Yes I will see you in the morning. (*He exits.*)

(*While leaving.*) Thank you Jesus, thank you Lord. No more pain, no more sinning, for Brother Harry.

DAVID: Goodnight.

JULIE: Goodnight. Well, David.

DAVID: Well David what? Please, I'm trying to think.

JULIE: Don't they know it's 1971? What do they take God for? Who started all this rubbish in Jamaica? No one would believe that they can read and write. Did they do this sort of thing in Jamaica? David, you are the one to be blamed for all this. Jesus Christ, they are beyond help. Why don't you say something?

DAVID: What do you want me to say? Please don't bother me. You still don't understand, do you?

JULIE: You're bloody right, I'm sure I don't understand. Oh fuck, why do you encourage them? I can't believe that you were one of them.

DAVID: Julie, don't make me lose my temper.

JULIE: And to think that I believed you love them. Don't you see they are all mad. I must see this church that George is talking about. As a matter of fact I think I'll go to his church.

DAVID: I wouldn't do that if I were you.

JULIE: Why not?

DAVID: They might convert you too.

JULIE: Oh shut up and try to make sense.

DAVID: You are really pushing your luck tonight.

JULIE: Don't it bother you to see George destroying all of them? I hope you will stand up for Castan.

DAVID: You want him to hate me for the rest of my life? I am glad George is staying here. Believe me there is hundreds like Brother George just waiting to take his place, and most of them are worse than George. I will tell you what I would like to do. Turn bloody history upside down. All Aunt Gloria and George want is love and friendship from other people. What the hell else can they do? Since they come to England all they do is go to work, come home and go back to work the fucking next morning.

JULIE: I am sorry David but...

DAVID: How the hell do you think I feel? I am going to tell you something. The man who owns this house is in the madhouse. You know why? He came to England and work for five years seven days a week in the fucking rubber factory. He also buy himself a car. He was one of the proudest man in England. He think he was the greatest and all his problem was solve for life. He was in bed one night when he heard people smashing his front door down. It was the police looking for two Jamaicans who they believe was selling drugs. They wasn't there that night. The poor fool jumps out of bed and start fighting the police and tried to throw them out of his house. They beat hell out of him and lock him up.

JULIE: How very sad. What do you expect if he starts fighting the police? A medal?

DAVID: So you are taking sides with the police now.

JULIE: No, but there is such a thing as the law.

DAVID: Don't you think I know that? But that's not the point. He believe they have no right to come in his house, and anyway he doesn't know a damned thing about drugs. I don't think he have ever even seen anyone smoking leaves. They keep him in prison for seven days and fine him 50 pounds. He came home and talk bloody rubbish for a month. He give up work and start living with a woman who hate the police anyway. He give her all his money. She only wanted the room so she could do business in it. The police came for him again. This time he get six month. He came home again and two weeks after that he was in a straightjacket.

JULIE: Well whose fault was that, and what do you mean she was doing business?

DAVID: That's alright, Julie. It is very good if you don't know what I mean by she was doing business, so forget it.

JULIE: Why should I forget it? I am involved with you, and God knows how long we'll be staying here for.

DAVID: Let's hope you don't have to do business.

JULIE: For God's sake, will you try and make sense?

DAVID: Just give me a chance to explain. Don't you realise by now that all they do is go to work and not a bloody thing else. So you see, my innocent, they don't know a damned thing what's going on around them. They are in love with one another.

JULIE: But I still don't see what all that has to do with putting fear into them about God.

DAVID: Well I would much rather George do what he's doing to them than the police coming back here, and believe me it's only going to be the police or God. They spend so much time in this fucking stinking house. They have always feel very free and move about a lot when they was in Jamaica. If they didn't go to church they would be having parties every day, and that is an open invitation for the police to search the house for drugs. Yes God I am happy for them. Where we come from every house have lawns with stones for chairs. Everybody meet on everybody lawn for a sing-song. Don't think that I am saying they are right, but it is very difficult to change grown men and women.

JULIE: Well I am not going to sit in this place and watch them punishing themselves. I am going to do something about it.

DAVID: What the hell can you do about it?
(*CASTAN enters.*)

CASTAN: Well it's rass cloth cold outside. I don't see why I should let a punk like that keep me out of here. I am putting George out tomorrow.

JULIE: Castan, what would you like us to do tomorrow? Let's all of us have a party. Come to think of it, it would be nice if nobody goes to work tomorrow.

DAVID: How comes Aunt Gloria is dying and nobody takes her to the doctor?

CASTAN: Well David, you know whose fault that is. Just look what happened tonight. We were just sitting down having a drink, George comes in, hit Gloria and set about fighting me and Harry. I bet the rass clath man wouldn't do that if we were sober. And the next thing I know George say him convert Harry, and then right in front of my eyes they start saying they are the Holy Ghost. I tell you David, Harry was drunk as rass. How can God possibly get in a drunken man? Now you see how wicked that man George is.

DAVID: I think it is very funny. Why didn't you tell him that Harry was drunk?

CASTAN: So tell me something. George blind? A wicked, the man, wicked. He want Harry to work for him.

JULIE: You should stop him. You are his friend and relation. It's up to you to help him.

CASTAN: Well God knows what's going to happen tomorrow when Harry wake up sober. I hope him kill George blood clath.

JULIE: I think things are getting very interesting. Yes my mind is made up. I am going to join George's church, so I will have to speak to him first.

DAVID: Good for you. Don't forget to pray for me.

CASTAN: Look Julie, you don't know what you saying. Anyway, it's not my business. You are David woman and it's up to him to put proper control over you.

JULIE: So you both don't see what I'm getting at. Well somebody's got to do something. David, you are going to take your auntie to the doctor in the morning aren't you?

CASTAN: I will have to go with you David. It's going to take both of us to get her to a doctor. I hope you realise that I am always trying to get Gloria to go to the doctor. She think God and rass clath George is going to cure her.

DAVID: Julie, I'm going to tell you something. Just watch what you are doing. There is enough trouble in the house already.

JULIE: What do you mean?

DAVID: You just watch it. That's all.

CASTAN: Come on David. Please, it look like we all going mad. I tell you man, it's that rass clath George. I hope you don't mind David, but if Julie can help us get that man out of this house and away from your aunt, it will be rass clath good.

JULIE: Can we go to bed now? I'm tired.

DAVID: You can go. I'm not ready yet.

JULIE: Acting the bloody fool again.

DAVID: One day I won't be able to control myself.

JULIE: Oh shut up, I'm not afraid of you any more. You're just a silly little coward. Goodnight.

(*JULIE exits. DAVID rushes after her.*)

CASTAN: (*Shouting.*) David don't.

DAVID: I think you better go to bed Castan.

CASTAN: Both of us better go to bed. Remember we both takin' Gloria to the doctor in the morning.

DAVID: Alright, but I just want to sit down here and think for a while.

(*CASTAN exits.*)

Curtain.

Next morning.

GLORIA: (*Talking to herself. Cleaning the floor.*) Lord what happen last night? I feel so run down. I will have a glass of my tonic. Lord my head is getting worse, and my back is killing me.

(*HARRY enters.*)

HARRY: Gloria, will you stop talking to yourself. If you feel sick why don't you go to the doctor?

GLORIA: I need no doctor. Look what you and Castan make me do last night. I hope you stay a good Christian and don't mock God.

HARRY: What do you mean, stay a good Christian?

GLORIA: Just what I said, stay a good Christian. I don't want God to put any more curse on the family.

HARRY: Gloria, I know you are talking to yourself, but I didn't know you was already completely mad. You know, it's a funny thing, I dream that David come home last night with his girlfriend. You know, I have a funny feeling he's alright in London.

GLORIA: Why you trying to put me in the madhouse? My own flesh and blood. You know David is home with his girlfriend, so don't try to get out of it. It's funny, you become a Christian and I become too weak to carry the cross.

HARRY: So tell me something, Gloria, when did you turn back from the road to heaven?

GLORIA: The same time you get me drunk and Castan try to sleep with me. I am not a fool, you know. Castan is after me.

HARRY: Gloria, what the hell got into you this morning? You have completely changed.

GLORIA: You cannot fool God, Harry, so don't make out you was too drunk last night. Everybody see you get the Holy Ghost right here in this house.

HARRY: Yes I remember now. We were all drinking last night and George came in and kicked the record player over. So tell me something. George convert me and Castan last night?

GLORIA: No, my beloved brother, just you.

HARRY: But where is Castan? Does he go to work on a Saturday?

GLORIA: I don't know. George must have put him out last night. He is probably at one of his women.

HARRY: But here my rass cloth trial. But I could be on a good thing with George. His church is getting richer every day. Maybe I was converted last night. Yes, Brother George, I am your man, and Barclays Bank is between us.

GLORIA: God will kill you for this, mark my word. You will eat your shit on your deathbed.

HARRY: Rass clath, I give up slave labour for blood clath white people.

(*DAVID enters.*)

DAVID: Morning, Uncle Harry, how do you feel after your wonderful change of life? Come on Aunt Gloria, we will be late for the doctor.

HARRY: David, isn't it wonderful? I receive the Holy Ghost. I am going to be Brother George right-hand man. I can serve him well.

GLORIA: Oh Lord, my head David. I can't go to the doctor. I have to stay with Harry. He needs all the help he can get.

DAVID: I understand, Aunt Gloria, but Castan and me are taking you to the doctor. Brother George will look after Brother Harry. They are both saints for the Lord now.

GLORIA: But you don't understand. Harry is mad.

(*CASTAN enters.*)

CASTAN: Are you ready David? Come on, Gloria, we'll be late.

GLORIA: You don't realise I have got to keep Harry away from Brother George.

HARRY: Alright, my lovely sister, if you feel that way I will come to the doctor with you.

CASTAN: Yes it is good to have a man of God with us when we go travelling.

GLORIA: No no no, I will go. Let us all go. What am I saying? My headache is getting worse. I don't sleep at all these days.

CASTAN: Don't worry, Gloria. We will take you to a good doctor. He come from Jamaica and everybody go to see him.

HARRY: Alright, alright. Let us get it over with. And I will also say a prayer for my dear sister on our way to the doctor.

GLORIA: Yes I know how much you hate me Harry.

DAVID: Aunt Gloria, please.

GLORIA: I am only going for David's sake. Well I am ready.

(*GLORIA, DAVID, HARRY and CASTAN exit. GEORGE*

enters singing, with his Bible in his hand. He sits down and
starts reading aloud. JULIE enters.)

JULIE: Good morning, Brother George.

GEORGE: Good morning, my child. Did you sleep well?

JULIE: Yes thank you. The house is very quiet this morning.
Where is everybody?

GEORGE: Yes, it seems so. I was about to ask the same
question myself.

JULIE: Oh yes, I remember now. They must have taken
Gloria to the doctor.

GEORGE: What in the name of God are you saying? Gloria
gone to the doctor? What is wrong with her? I suppose
she's been sinning again. Yes Lord, I have done my part.
I cannot do any more. My prayers are not good enough
for her anymore. Yes it is the Lord will she should be
punish. When men have done their best angel cannot do
any more.

JULIE: Do you believe God is punishing her?

GEORGE: Oh yes, I do. Only last night I caught her
sinning with that evil Castan. But God is wise and
wonderful. I was able to save Harry soul last night.

JULIE: Yes I see what you mean, and that is very good.

GEORGE: Thank you my child.

JULIE: Were they making love when you caught them?

GEORGE: Do you mean having sexual intercourse?

JULIE: Yes.

GEORGE: Well, no, but they were drinking and dancing.

JULIE: And I suppose that is extremely wrong in the eyes
of God?

GEORGE: Oh yes, my child, very wrong. And I hope you
also realise what would have happen if I did not stop
them. That evil Castan would have end up sleeping in
her bed.

JULIE: Yes that would be very disastrous. I feel very hot.
I think I might be having a temperature. (*She takes her
dressing-gown off.*) Tell me, Brother George, does your
religion allow you to get married?

GEORGE: Well yes, but I have to wait on Jesus to choose the right woman for me. No my child, I have no time for worldly pleasures.

JULIE: I would like to come to your church one day, but David is such a little boy, he might stop me from coming. I would really like to hear you preach.

GEORGE: Please do not let David stop you. You must insist. Come tomorrow.

JULIE: That's what I like, a real man. (*She sits next to GEORGE*.) You're a great man, Brother George, and I like you. Yes, my mind is made up. I will come to your church.

GEORGE: Bless your saintly heart, my child.

JULIE: That's alright. Can I call you George?

GEORGE: Well nobody calls me George, but you could call me Deacon.
(*JULIE puts her hand on GEORGE's knee. GEORGE stands up and sits down again*.)

JULIE: (*Hands moving across his legs*.) Well, Deacon, what about it?

GEORGE: Lord have mercy. I'm only human.

JULIE: That's right, Deacon. I am also human too, and I needed you from the moment I set eyes on you.
(*Her hands everywhere*.) I like a real man. Look at the way you handle Castan, Harry and Gloria, and David is such a little boy. They are all afraid of you because you are so powerful and great. Come on, Deacon, make love to me.

GEORGE: Oh Lord have mercy. No, my child, God will never forgive us. We will burn in hell. A saint cannot make love. Please let me pray for you. (*He gets on his knees*.) Oh Lord.
(*JULIE climbs on him*.)

JULIE: Come on, Deacon, fuck me.

GEORGE: Fuck you? What is happening to me? The flesh is very weak.

JULIE: That's right, George baby, I am going to die if I don't get it.

GEORGE: Yes Lord, mercy mercy. (*He starts undoing his trousers*.)

JULIE: Yes, yes, I love you.

(*GEORGE grabs her. His trousers fall around his ankles.*)

Come on, Deacon.

(*They fall on the floor.*)

GEORGE: Yes I am coming.

JULIE: (*Screaming.*) Get your hands off me, you stinking horrible bastard. (*She slaps his face and kicks him.*) Just look at you. David is going to kill you. And what about the rest of the family and your bloody precious church? (*She puts on her dressing-gown.*) What about the church, eh Brother George? You are right, the flesh is very weak. (*JULIE laughs, GEORGE starts thumping the floor.*) Look at the crawling bastard.

(*GLORIA and HARRY enter.*)

GLORIA: (*Shouting.*) I am not going to hospital. Nothing is wrong with me. Lord God almighty, what the rass cloth you think you doing George?

HARRY: But George a so you wicked. You take away young David woman.

JULIE: Well not really. He is very weak for the flesh. I think he's a sinner as from now.

(*GEORGE stands up, zips his trousers and walks out.*)

GLORIA: Well, Julie. Lord God, my head.

JULIE: No no, he didn't. He is useless anyway. Where is David?

HARRY: But what have my eye witnessed? What about my place in the church? Jesus Christ, I will have to go back to rass cloth slave labour.

GLORIA: No Lord, I don't believe my eyes. Brother George who I take in this house trying to go to bed with my sister son woman. I shall never walk the street again. Shame, shame on the whole family. Yes my mind is made up. I am going to hospital and I am never going to come out again.

JULIE: Please, where is David?

HARRY: He went with Castan across the road. We didn't get to the doctor. Gloria think they would put her in the hospital.

GLORIA: You see what I mean, Harry? One mind was saying to me before I go in to see the doctor that he would put me in hospital, and that's why I couldn't go in, and just look what I leave Jamaica to come and witness. The man was a sex maniac all the time. Oh God, how I love that man. Now I'll never get out the hospital.

HARRY: I still can't believe it. Me soul bottom drop right out of me belly bottom.

JULIE: Gloria, have you ever told George that you love him?

GLORIA: No my child. You don't tell a holy man like the deacon that you love them. There is no place in their life for a woman.

JULIE: I think he needs you now. Well, you've just seen him with his trousers down.

HARRY: Julie, I am not a fool. You know I can't help thinking that you purposely do this to George. David is a ignorant man. He will surely murder him rass cloth.

JULIE: Please, does David have to know about this? Nothing happened anyway. Please no more trouble.

GLORIA: Where did George go? What about his new church? All gone on my sister son woman. Yes Lord, the world is bound to change. Harry, do you think I should go and look for George?

HARRY: Gloria, don't you realise what happen today?

JULIE: I told you, nothing happened. He just proved himself to be human.

GLORIA: I still don't believe it. Look how long the man never look at me as a woman. Harry, David and Castan must never know about this.

JULIE: Please Gloria, go and look for him.

HARRY: I don't understand you, Julie. Am I dreaming or what? Tell me something, what really happen here today?

GLORIA: Please child, save me the pain. Don't say nothing or I will drop dead. I am going to look for George. Well bless my soul, my headache is gone. (*She exits.*)

HARRY: (*Laughing.*) Jesus Christ, I'm going to leave the house before anybody else comes in. What a rass cloth when David find out.

(*DAVID and CASTAN enter.*)

DAVID: Why haven't you dressed, Julie? It's almost one o'clock.

HARRY: Well David my son, there are more than one reason to your question.

CASTAN: I see you still drunk, Harry man, or is it the Holy Ghost that is talking.

JULIE: I think I will go and change. (*She exits.*)

DAVID: Well Uncle Harry, what exactly do you mean?

HARRY: Well I think she change the deacon.

CASTAN: I know that would happen. That rass clath is not satisfied with Gloria. He got to have young David one as well.

DAVID: Will you shut up Castan. What the hell been going on here Harry between Julie and George?

HARRY: I see, so I'm not your uncle any more. I am just plain old Harry. Tell you the truth, David, I don't know where to start from.

DAVID: Lord God, I am having headache as well. I don't believe it. (*Shouting.*) Julie, come on down here immediately.

CASTAN: Where's George?

HARRY: Well, when I saw him last he was a quiet as a lamb, so I suppose he's with his flock. Lord God, hard work again on Monday morning.

DAVID: I don't care a rass clath. The time has come for me to say my piece in this house. First before I kill Julie or George I want some facts from you Harry, and no rass clath kid's stuff. Castan, go and look for George. Lord God, I don't want to find him first. (*Shouting.*) Julie, bring your rass clath self down here.

HARRY: Now, David, nothing happen as far as I know and as far as I am concerned. This is too much for me. Then perhaps the time has come for me to part company with my own flesh and blood.

CASTAN: Lord God almighty, George never stop until he bring murder in the house.

DAVID: Castan, what are you waiting for? Go and look for George.

CASTAN: Alright, David, but remember that I am a big man and I also have my problems with George. (*He exits.*)

DAVID: Alright Harry, start talking. Don't think you can fool me with this holy shit stuff. I know you was drunk last night, and remember I have more sense than you. You're all stupid in this house. I hope James comes out of the madhouse and throw the fucking lot of you out.

HARRY: That's enough, David. Since you're a big man, as you claim to be, you solve your own problem. Go and kill George if you like, I don't care. Don't think I don't know about you. I bet you didn't sing in any nightclub. I suppose you only come back because the police was after you.

DAVID: I see what you mean. Because you think you is a Christian you take side with George and then you start talking about singing and the police. I don't care what you say, I just want to find out about Julie and George. Haven't you got any shame, Uncle Harry? What do you want me to do?

(*JULIE enters.*)

HARRY: Julie, there's going to be big trouble before the day finish, so please tell your punk friend here that I am a big man and I know nothing about what happen here today.

DAVID: What were you doing upstairs? I call you six times and you take no notice. Since you come here you cause nothing but trouble. Up to last night I was warning you, but you take no notice. Well start talking, and remember you can't fool me.

JULIE: Start talking about what?

DAVID: So you don't know what I am talking about? I better beat out the baby out of your belly that you say is mine.

JULIE: Oh God I wish you would do that. Then I would be free again. This is a prison full of all mad people. I have nothing but pain since I knew you and came to this house.

HARRY: What is this I am listening to? No I am not a Christian. I am going down the pub to get drunk. The little boy is going to be a father. What a day.

DAVID: Julie, I don't care what you say, and you better explain because if George went to bed with you I am going to kill the both of you today. You rass cloth.

HARRY: That's right, big man. Kill her. I don't care. She is your woman. When the police finish with you the judge will take care of you and then you will have to answer to God. Boy, times really change. (*He exits.*)

JULIE: Are you satisfied now? You can kill me if you like, I don't care. I knew you were a woman-beater before I went out with you. You don't care about anything or anybody. You're in love with yourself, and all I have to say to you is that nothing happened between me and George, and I think you have gone far enough so please forget it.

DAVID: You want me to forget it? You are the only woman I ever loved in the whole world. I would give my life for you. I came home today and everybody start acting strange and then they say something about you and George, my own woman in my family house. What am I supposed to do?

JULIE: Well, for a start get your facts straight. First, how you could believe that I would go to bed with George I do not know. He is old enough to be my father.

DAVID: That's exactly what I mean. That's why I went mad. How could you possibly do that to me?

JULIE: Look, all I did today was tease George a little. Maybe I was wrong, I don't know, but you must admit that George has a great hold on your whole family. I am sure George thought that he was above ordinary people. I just wanted to show him that he wasn't.

DAVID: Oh Julie, when will you ever learn? They all love one another. They have lived like that all their lives and they will spend the rest of their life like that.

JULIE: How can you say that? You saw what Castan was like last night, and just look at your Aunt Gloria. I am sorry, I thought it was my duty to do something.

DAVID: Please listen very carefully to what I am going to say. Since the day I can remember they all take it in turns to be Christians. Every so often when they get fed

up or do something which they think is wrong they
become Christian and they never last for more than a
couple of months at a time. Gloria, Castan, Harry, even
my own mother in Jamaica, they are all the same. One
day they have the Holy Ghost and the next day they are
sinners again. But you see, their Brother George have
always remain a Christian, and that is the only reason
why they respect him, and as you rightly say are also
afraid of him.

JULIE: David, I am sorry. Why didn't you say this before?

DAVID: You will never know how much you hurt George.
His only pride and glory. You completely destroyed him.
All he live for is to tell people how he have always been
a Christian and never look back since he take up the
Bible and start serving God. I feel sorry for him.
I wouldn't be surprised if we find him hanging by his
neck from some tree.

JULIE: I think I will have nightmares for the rest of my
life. This is like a bad dream.

DAVID: He is sure to join James in the madhouse. If his
own innocent flock don't kill him. If they find out about
this and yet nothing happens like you said, I hope Castan
find him before he goes mad and do something stupid.

JULIE: But Castan hates him. Surely he's only looking for
him to fight him. You must realise that when you sent
him out to look for him.

DAVID: You must be joking. They will all become Christians
again because right now they all will be feeling sorry for
George. You can read them like a book. Maybe that's why
I love them.

JULIE: I don't think I'll ever understand. Even you have
changed since we started talking. David, you know I love
you. I only wish I could understand.

DAVID: I hate to say this, but I did warn you, and believe
me it is only hard to understand because there is nothing
to understand. They are just simple people who is hard
outside but very soft inside. Their biggest problem is
love for their friends and above all they want to be
friends with everybody and for others to love them.

JULIE: Stop. You're breaking my heart. I will start crying in a minute. Oh God, I feel sick.

DAVID: I am sorry Julie, I feel the same way myself.

JULIE: I still say they go the hard way about simple things.

DAVID: Yes, you may be right, but I don't think they know any other way.

JULIE: Whose fault is that?

DAVID: I am sure you could answer that better than myself.

JULIE: You make me want to hate myself. I don't know what you mean.

DAVID: Come on, Julie, don't be stupid.

JULIE: I know I was wrong with George, and I am truly sorry, but for a minute I thought you were blaming me for something else.

DAVID: I am sorry, Julie. Please remember that I love you too.

JULIE: I still say you need a computer to have the faintest idea what's going on.
(*CASTAN enters.*)

CASTAN: David, I don't care and I don't care if you kill me, but oh Lord forgive me. I went out this house today with vengeance in my heart for George and I look everywhere for him and I couldn't find him. I even went to where Brother Clifford live and some of the people who belong to his church. I couldn't find him anywhere, and then one kind say to me, 'Why don't you go and look for him in the church.' I don't know why, but it was like some spirit was leading me, and there he was in church crying, bawling and rolling all over the place, begging to God for forgiveness. I tell you, David, I really feel sorry for him. I nearly start crying. I couldn't say anything to him. I have to run out the church.

JULIE: Please David, I am sorry. Can I go and lay down upstairs? (*She exits.*)

DAVID: I wonder how Aunt Gloria feeling. I better tell her to go and look for him.

CASTAN: No, it's alright. I see her down the road looking for him after I run out of the church. She has gone to him. She start crying right in the middle of the road when I tell her. I tell you, David boy, life really tough. I wonder what really happen today.

DAVID: Julie said nothing happens, and before you say anything, I believe her.

CASTAN: Look, David, you don't know how glad I am to hear that. But Julie looks so upset when I start talking.

DAVID: You know these people don't understand anything.

CASTAN: Yes I know what you mean. Boy, I think I will go and take a drink. I need it. Kiss my rass cloth, if Harry didn't turn Christian last night me and him could go for a drink.

DAVID: Don't worry Castan, he's a sinner again. I heard him swearing when you left. He's down the pub drinking right now.

CASTAN: Thank God for that. But David, we haven't have a drink together since you came home. What you say we go for a drink?

DAVIID: Alright, Castan. But let me say something for a minute. You know it's really funny, but I came home to celebrate and I really think everybody would be alright. You see, Julie is going to have a baby and I am sure I love her. You know what I mean.

CASTAN: Yes David, I know what you mean, and I understand. Boy, it's good to see you thinking about settling down. Listen man, what do you say we go out and bring the drinks back so we could sit down and talk, and anyway I prefer to drink in the house.

DAVID: You know, Castan, I could never make a singer. I think I could until I went to London, but there's hundred of singer better than me in London starving. If it wasn't for Julie I suppose I would drop dead with hunger up there. Boy, I was really glad to get back home. Come on, let's go and get the drinks.

(DAVID and CASTAN exit, GLORIA and GEORGE enter.)

GEORGE: I am deeply sorry, Sister Gloria. You must also believe me as God is my witness, nothing happen.

GLORIA: Brother George, please, I know you are telling
the truth. I know you far too long not to believe you.
Remember I just finish praying with you in church.
The way you were praying I am sure Jesus heard you,
and I know he forgive you.

GEORGE: Yes, I have to change my whole life. Start all
over again. I am prepared to take my punishment. I must
apologise to the young lady. What a fool I am. I am
going to fast and pray for a whole month. If David try to
kill me I shall not lift a finger to stop him. I only hope
he doesn't get into trouble for it. The judge will have to
understand that it was my fault. He cannot send him to
prison for beating hell out of me. I know God will
forgive him and that is very good. I don't think I can
live this day out.

GLORIA: Brother George, please don't worry. I will stand
by you until the day of judgement. You have always
stand by me in my time of troubles. And think of the
hundreds of people soul you have saved. Think how they
all love you. Nothing happen, so they will have to forget
it. Is my sister only son, but he can't do you anything.

GEORGE: My road is going to be much harder, but I will
never give up. Jesus will have to give me more strength
if I pray hard enough. Lord Jesus, I am praying like
I never pray before.

(*HARRY enters, drinking.*)

HARRY: George, you praying? David bust your rass cloth
head when he sees you. But George, I didn't know you
like young girl. Boy, life is really funny. I didn't know
you could do it.

GLORIA: Harry, God will strike you dead for this.

HARRY: So be it. I am not a big man. So tell me something,
I can't talk if I want to. After all, it's not right for a man to
go through life without breaking his water.

GLORIA: Harry, leave the house before I kill you, you
drunken old nigger.

HARRY: Hold your tongue, sister. The devil must be
rejoicing in hell today. A man who never smoke and

never drink, but he take a woman to hand over his soul for ever and ever to the devil. It's been a great day for the devil. I wish I did see you George, breaking your water. You must a nicka like some old horse. Your water run like river, eh George?

GLORIA: Somebody stop me before I kill him.

GEORGE: Please, Sister Gloria, it is the Lord punishment, and it is not as heavy as the cross that Jesus carry for sinners.

HARRY: Boy, things really funny. You save my soul last night and then you lost me right back to the devil next day. So tell me something George, David hasn't seen you yet?

GLORIA: I am warning you Harry.

GEORGE: No, I haven't seen David.

GLORIA: I suppose they are out getting drunk like you.

HARRY: Well, I think I'll go and look for them. Get back praying, Brother George, but I have a funny feelings prayer won't save you this time. Raping the innocent boy woman.

(*GLORIA starts screaming, HARRY runs out.*)

GLORIA: Brother George, take no notice. That brother of mine is a fool when he's drunk. Please Brother George, Jesus already forgive you. Think of your church and how many people soul you have put in heaven.

GEORGE: Thank you. You give me much strength. But I have been thinking, and if David doesn't kill me, and I must admit I am weak to the flesh, I think the time has come for me to start looking for a woman. Maybe a man should have a wife.

GLORIA: Please don't torture yourself any more today.

GEORGE: Please listen, Sister Gloria.

GLORIA: Brother George, I really can't listen. You deserve somebody much better than me. I am sure I'm not good enough for you.

GEORGE: Sister Gloria; will you marry me?

GLORIA: Oh, my poor dead mother. I think my bad back and headache is coming on again. I can't believe it. I will

not live this day out. Yes, Brother George, I will marry
you, in hell or in heaven. Lord I am so happy.
(*GLORIA starts crying. JULIE enters.*)

JULIE: Oh Gloria, what's the matter? Please don't cry.
(*She embraces GLORIA.*)

GLORIA: Please, it's not often I beg people for mercy, but
I am begging you now. Please forgive Brother George.
Please search your heart for mercy.

JULIE: Please, you must believe me, I have never felt more
rotten in my life. (*She goes over to GEORGE.*) Please
forgive me. I am truly sorry.

GEORGE: Heavenly joy to all the people of the world.
No my child, it is me who need your forgiveness.
(*He falls on his knees.*) I need forgiveness from you and
also from God. I was much too weak for a man who has
been serving God for such a long time.

GLORIA: Amen.

JULIE: I hope you will continue with the church. After all
nothing happened. I was just a bitch. (*She takes his hand.*)
Please don't do that. Stand up.

GLORIA: Yes Lord, the power and the glory and the Holy
Ghost, thank you child. I must also say that you are the first
one to know. Me and George are getting married as soon
as possible. Yes, we will continue with the church. It will
be the best church in the world. You will be proud of us.

JULIE: Well, that's fantastic. I am really happy for you two.
I also have something to tell you. I am having David's
baby. This calls for a celebration. Oh I am sorry, here
I go again, putting my foot in it. I am sorry.

GLORIA: Oh no, no, please we understand.

JULIE: I'm sure David won't mind, but you see he was very
unhappy in London. We were planning to get married,
but he couldn't go through with it before he got
permission from all of you. We also would like to get
married soon.

GLORIA: Well that's very good. Of course you have all of
us permission and blessing, but I can't believe my sister
is going to be a grandmother. Oh Lord, she will walk

very proud in Jamaica. Brother George, we must write a letter to her soon and tell her the good news.

JULIE: Oh thank you very much, but I suppose David will tell her about it himself.

GLORIA: I know my sister would like you. She is a good sister. Pity she is not in England. I am sure you would like her. Still, who knows, you might meet her one day. (*DAVID, CASTAN and HARRY enter, all carrying bottles. GLORIA and GEORGE grab each other.*)

GEORGE: Kill me if you like, David, I want no mercy for myself. I deserve a good beating. I shall do nothing to defend myself, and may the Lord have pity on both of us.

GLORIA: David, please my sister only son, I am your aunt, Harry your uncle, Castan your cousin, here is your lovely girl who love you very much. Your poor mother is still in Jamaica. I am a sick woman. Have mercy on George. Kill the both of us together. Please remember how much we all love you when you was a little boy. Nothing happens between Julie and Brother George.

GEORGE: That's right David, but I am still very much ashamed. I haven't stop crying. I was wrong. Oh I am so weak, words is failing me. There is pain in my heart. I have disgrace God and the whole world. I will never stop paying for my sin from this day on.

DAVID: What are you two talking about? I am glad to see you alright, Brother George. You're a good man. (*GLORIA can't believe it, claps her hands and grabs DAVID.*)

GLORIA: David, me and George getting married next Sunday.

CASTAN: But George, you really lucky you know.

HARRY: Well, thank God for that.

JULIE: Oh I am so glad.

DAVID: Well, I might as well say my piece. Me and Julie also getting married soon. That was the reason why we came home.

GLORIA: Yes I know David. She is very nice. She gave me and George great encouragement.

DAVID: Did she tell you everything?

GLORIA: Yes, I'm writing a letter to your mother telling her all about it.

CASTAN: George, you should thank your lucky stars. I hope you know that it is me who explain everything to David.

GEORGE: Let us all kneel in prayer.

HARRY: George, shut your rass clath. Let's have a drink. My sister is getting married.

JULIE: I don't believe it. One minute you're all killing each other, the next minute you're the greatest of friends.

CASTAN: It will give me great pleasure to pour you a drink, George. You have proven that you're a man.

HARRY: But wait a minute. So Brother George, all that money you have been putting in Barclays Bank, it all belongs to you now. It is good to have you as my brother-in-law. We will buy the rass clath house off James if he ever gets out the madhouse.

GEORGE: Look David, I have sinned today like I have never sinned before. If it would do any good, I would chop my right hand off.

CASTAN: It's your rass clath cock you want to chop off.

GLORIA: Shut up, Castan, this got nothing to do with you.

HARRY: But you are wrong, Gloria, this got everything to do with all of us.

GLORIA: My own brother against me in a time like this.

CASTAN: Well, I wasn't going to say anything, but the man is a pussy clath. Look how many woman he got in his church, and if anybody go near one of them he would surely burn their house down.

HARRY: A truth Castan a talk. He got some nice young girl in his church. Then tell me something, George, why didn't you grab one of them?

GLORIA: You see what I mean? None of you know George. George love me and no one else.

(*CASTAN and HARRY start laughing.*)

JULIE: (*Shouting.*) Shut up, the lot of you. I am sick, sick to the teeth. How can you live together like this? I don't know. The lot of you are like kids playing cowboys and Indians. What are you people running away from? Why can't you face facts? Nothing happened between me and George, and will you please stop using me as an excuse for your own childish ways. You are all just looking to each other for pity. George and Gloria are going to be married. They told me so today. I am having David's baby. We too are getting married. Those are the facts. (*Silence. EVERYBODY looks at JULIE.*)

CASTAN: I think I'll take a walk down the bookie. You coming Harry?

DAVID: Come on, Castan and Harry, we're all going to have a drink in a minute.

GEORGE: Please forgive me, but I feel very dirty. I have got to pray for guidance. I am very confused.

CASTAN: I know you, George. Now that we are on speaking terms, so you don't want to marry Gloria?

GLORIA: Castan, why do you always jump to conclusions.

HARRY: Now, George, Gloria is a big woman, but she's still my sister.

GEORGE: I am still a man of God. I will pray for all of you.

CASTAN: That's alright, but marry Gloria first, and then you can start praying for us again.

JULIE: Now what is the matter?

GLORIA: If anybody in this house doubt Brother George word God will punish all your souls in hell.

DAVID: Quiet, every one of you. We are going to have a drink, all of us. Julie, go in the kitchen and get some glasses. Let's get the record player.

HARRY: It's not working.

CASTAN: George break it up last night.

DAVID: That's alright, we got plenty of booze for everybody. We have got a lot to celebrate today.
(*JULIE enters with glasses, gay and very happy.*)

CASTAN: Come on, George, have a drink. You did well for yourself today.

GEORGE: I haven't had a drink for years.

HARRY: Come on, Gloria, get your husband to have a drink.
(*JULIE pours drinks for everybody.*)

CASTAN: Give George a drink. Yes George, my man, you're one of us now, so please finish the day with us.

You can go back to God tomorrow.

(*GEORGE refuses the drink.*)

GLORIA: Don't you realise his people need him for the church?

CASTAN: Which church? But wait, don't you think they know all about what happen here this morning? Everybody was talking about it down the shop. I don't know which one of us let it slip out.

JULIE: Please, please, anything else. Not again. The same bloody thing.

GLORIA: I don't believe you, Castan. You are still jealous of Brother George. I know you have always want to go to bed with me.

HARRY: So wait a minute, Gloria. Why do you think I was telling George about the money in Barclays Bank?

DAVID: It is true, Aunt Gloria, everybody thinks Brother George run away with the money. We nearly get in a fight about it.

GEORGE: So that's what they are saying about me.

DAVID: I am sorry there's nothing we could do about it.

GLORIA: Have faith, Brother George, Jesus will pull you through.

GEORGE: So far thirty years I work for the church and this is the thanks I get. Castan, get me that rass cloth drink and be quick about it.

(*EVERYBODY freezes.*)

GLORIA: No, Brother George.

(*HARRY grabs a bottle of whisky.*)

GEORGE: Quiet woman. What are you waiting for, Castan? Give me that drink. I'll show them.

CASTAN: Yes sir.

(*HARRY rushes to him with the bottle and the glass.*)

HARRY: Hallelujah. (*He starts pouring GEORGE drinks.*)
(*JULIE starts laughing, GLORIA buries her face in her hands, GEORGE knocks his whisky straight back. HARRY fills the glass again.*)

GEORGE: Since that day my mother die I never look back. Look how many people are in heaven because of me.

GLORIA: Brother George, please.

GEORGE: I told you to shut up, woman.

HARRY: That's right, Brother George, you tell her.

(*HARRY keeps filling the glass as fast as GEORGE knocks them back.*)

CASTAN: Lord the chicken is coming home to roost.

GEORGE: I have work day and night for the church and those evil people that I put into heaven. God must show them right into hell and let the devil have their souls. All those people who belongs to my church, they will all die very soon.

(*DAVID and JULIE exit.*)

I curse every one of them. They will regret turning their back on me.

(*HARRY hands him the bottle.*)

I shall build the biggest church in the world.

(*CASTAN and HARRY exit.*)

GLORIA: Yes, Brother George, I know your will.

GEORGE: Thousands of people shall follow me. I shall travel the whole country. (*He falls to the floor.*) They will regret putting their evil tongue on me. Kill all of them, Lord.

(*GEORGE starts crying. GLORIA falls next to him.*)

I want the biggest and the best church in the world. Lord, you must destroy all my enemies.

GLORIA: Yes, Brother George, Lord have mercy.

GEORGE: I am the best Christian ever lived. Nobody preach like me. (*He starts hitting the floor with the bottle, throws the glass away and become quite insane.*) Lord have mercy, I want a big church. I can see a multitude of people following me. My enemies shall not have me, I am protected by the Spirit and by millions of people. Amen. Hallelujah. Fire in front of my eyes. The rivers are on fire. Stop, I will not drown myself.

GLORIA: Yes Brother George.

GEORGE: Yes Lord, you save me from drowning again. Hallelujah. Amen. Praise be His name. Yes Lord I am getting the message. (*He stands up, arms open, looking up.*)

I must not let the devil take over your church yes God, I will do it. Burn the church down.

(*GLORIA stands up.*)

GLORIA: No Brother George, we are getting married.

GEORGE: Yes, God, I will do it today.

(*GEORGE grabs paraffin heater. GLORIA grabs GEORGE.*)

GLORIA: Stop, we are getting married. (*She hangs on to GEORGE.*)

GEORGE: No God, the Devil cannot stop me burn all of them with the church. Yes I am coming.

(*GEORGE exits with paraffin heater. GLORIA hangs onto him crying, screaming, begging.*)

(*Shouting off.*) Power, yes it is a great power.

The End.

THE DEATH OF A BLACK MAN

Characters

SHAKIE
aged 18

JACKIE
aged 30

STUMPIE
aged 21

The Death of a Black Man was first performed at the Hampstead Theatre as a Foco Novo production in 1975, with the following cast:

SHAKIE,   Gregory Munro

JACKIE,   Mona Hammond

STUMPIE,   Anton Phillips

Director,   Roland Rees

Designer,   Bernard Culshaw

ACT ONE

The play is set in Chelsea. The flat is furnished in Habitat style.

SHAKIE standing in the middle of the room, holding a cricket bat like a machine gun dressed in army uniform.

SHAKIE: Poi! Poi! Ratatatata! Shoot them down! God blind me. Sobers would lick them for six, every rass ball from the nursery end. Cricket, lovely cricket! (*He shapes himself as Sobers making some fine stroke.*) If Sobers was American, he'd be a better baseball player than Willie Mayes. God blind my days! When Sobers is fielding he catch so many balls, anyone would think he was Gordon Banks in goal playing for England. Pelé should have been a cricketer. Just imagine Pelé and Sobers at Lords! It would be six runs every time the Englishman bowled from the nursery end. By the centre, QUICK MARCH! Pelé shoots from fifty yards…it's a GOAL! Fire for you – Sobers hit another six. Black people jumping for joy all over England. Black people is the best cricketers in the world, and Sobers is their captain. Garfield Sobers break records every day that he plays cricket. My number is 23676752 and I rather watch Sobers play cricket on Sunday, Sa! August Bank Holiday 1973, the same day Sobers win the test for the West Indies is the same day Ladbroke Grove witnessed the greatest carnival England ever seen. The popular people were out of the street enjoying themselves, men, women, children and babies. Down Ladbroke Grove which is quite near Notting Hill Gate, which is almost in the centre of London, thousands of black people were singing, dancing and clapping in carnival in the streets of Ladbroke Grove. Boy, cricket, lovely cricket! I must get myself a new uniform. This damn khaki uniform is scratching me in the wrong places. I will have to get a new uniform that makes me look like Sobers hitting sixes all over Lords.

(*SHAKIE puts the cricket bat between his legs and poses like a horse and jockey flicking his finger. JACKIE enters, stands in doorway.*)

JACKIE: Little boy blue, you sure talk a lot of shit! Can I come in?

SHAKIE: What for?

JACKIE: Not even glad to see me?

SHAKIE: I am flabbergasted.

JACKIE: Don't worry, I'm on holiday. Only passing through. Two years ago was the last time I saw you.

SHAKIE: It was the same time I last saw you too.

JACKIE: Come off your high ass baby.

SHAKIE: How did you know where to find me?

JACKIE: It's very easy to follow the trail of a traitor.

SHAKIE: How is the baby?

JACKIE: Piss off! What baby? What do you care what happens to her? Priscilla is fine, she's in Paris with my boyfriend.

SHAKIE: So you live in Paris now?

JACKIE: No, Eastbourne.

SHAKIE: The same thing. They are close enough. I never believe you would leave the King's Road and the Chelsea set.

JACKIE: Is this your place?

SHAKIE: Yes.

JACKIE: Nice.

SHAKIE: So what are you doing in Eastbourne? I suppose you are still rich?

JACKIE: Honest social work for the council.

SHAKIE: My God, you have turned into a saint! Your dad still support you?

JACKIE: No I do it myself.

SHAKIE: Your boyfriend is rich then?

JACKIE: No, he's a retired schoolmaster with a cottage in the country.

SHAKIE: Holy father! You're really tripping out! Double freak. You either screw old men or little boys.

JACKIE: Why not? They have a lot in common.

SHAKIE: You are now a fully fledged English wench! So what brought you to London?

JACKIE: You.

SHAKIE: Me?

JACKIE: Yes.

SHAKIE: How very interesting. Well, what can I do for you?

JACKIE: Nothing.

SHAKIE: Thank God for that! Would you like a drink?

JACKIE: Yes, what have you got?

SHAKIE: Champagne.

JACKIE: Champagne?

SHAKIE: Yes, and the best. (*He pours out two glasses of champagne from an already half-empty bottle.*)

JACKIE: I thought you were still selling Scottish Best Peat Water to the American tourists down King's Road.

SHAKIE: I got promoted. I am now importing African art and crafts.

JACKIE: So you are still down Carnaby Street?

SHAKIE: No, King's Road. But I am keeping an eye on the Portobello Road. That's a road with a lot of a future.

JACKIE: Why are you interested in Portobello Road? You are getting ready to rob poor black people?

SHAKIE: Partly. But there is more to it.

JACKIE: So where is she then?

SHAKIE: Who?

JACKIE: Wife, girlfriend, I don't know.

SHAKIE: I live on my own as usual. Do you remember Stumpie?

JACKIE: How could I forget him. You talk about him enough.

SHAKIE: I expect him back from Germany this week. He might share the flat with me.

JACKIE: Oh, so you are still friends then?

SHAKIE: Of course.

JACKIE: Mind you, he is less eccentric than yourself. (*SHAKIE pours more champagne into her glass.*) Thanks. Come on, tell me about your girlfriend.

SHAKIE: What girlfriend? You still nosy as ever. I haven't got a girlfriend.

JACKIE: Bloody liar.

SHAKIE: Tell me about Priscilla.

JACKIE: She's grown quite a bit since we last saw you.

SHAKIE: Is your retired schoolteacher an Englishman?

JACKIE: Yes. Why? He's also Jewish. Jealous baby?

SHAKIE: Yes.

JACKIE: God, you fucking wicked bastard.

SHAKIE: When did they go to Paris?

JACKIE: Three days ago.

SHAKIE: So that give you a chance to find me?

JACKIE: Yes.

SHAKIE: You look as sexy as ever.

JACKIE: Forget it. I am not going to screw you.

SHAKIE: Who said anything about screwing you?

JACKIE: You forget I know you. Why are you saying I look sexy?

SHAKIE: I think you should treat my remark about you looking sexy as a compliment.

JACKIE: You are too wicked to pay a compliment to anybody. You are getting ready to rape me! Like you have always done in the past.

SHAKIE: When did I ever rape you?

JACKIE: You tricked me every time.

SHAKIE: Didn't you enjoy it?

JACKIE: Once. The first time.

SHAKIE: You must be freaking out the Monday Club members in the Conservative Party in Eastbourne.

JACKIE: I am a respectable social worker. Why do you hate women? I could never tell if you are a queer or not.

SHAKIE: A queer, eh? Why, because you are a lesbian?

JACKIE: Me a lesbian? Don't make me laugh!

SHAKIE: So why are you such a fucking freak? You only screw old men or little boys.

JACKIE: Emotional security, that's all.

SHAKIE: I hope Priscilla don't follow in your footsteps.

JACKIE: Stop trying to be dirty.

SHAKIE: What sort of fellow is this schoolteacher of yours?

JACKIE: That is my business. Why are you wearing that stupid army uniform? When did you take up cricket? Haven' you got any more clothes?

SHAKIE: No. Are you going to buy me some nice suit darling? Cricket, lovely cricket! Lick them blood clath Sobers! Yes I have changed my ways and habits. Take the army uniform off my back. Marry you for the good upbringing of Priscilla.

JACKIE: God almighty! What a fucking wicked freak you are. Cricket bat with army uniform! You will be raping little boys next. You talk pure shit. You are sick, very sick. You can't even have a normal discussion like normal people.

SHAKIE: What's normal about me?

JACKIE: Absolutely nothing, little boy blue.

SHAKIE: Well then. Lick them rass clath Sobers! I am going to sell the continent of Africa to the Americans and make enough money to keep Priscilla in luxury.

JACKIE: What am I supposed to say? Thank you? Oh, my God, I should be crying, tears running down my eyes! Me, a big 30-year-old woman allowing a 15-year-old boy to screw me in the middle of England and give me a baby. I remember quite clearly when you drive the last nail into my heart to kill me. Before I screws you you told me you were twenty-one. So, in my final humiliation to my family, I sue you for maintenance. It was headlines in all the newspapers! 'Twenty-eight year-old woman sues 15-year-old boy for maintenance.' How was I to know you was only 15?

(*SHAKIE pours more champagne into her glass.*)

Look at you. Eighteen, and you look a grey wreck old man of 35. I don't care how many times you sell the continent of Africa to the American tourists. You will never have a penny for yourself, you are too stupid, thief and wicked! Boy, I have to laugh! You at 16 open the first water bar, selling London stinking water to poor American tourists! You are heartless, fatherless and motherless.

SHAKIE: If people can go to health farms and spend hundreds of pounds for the pleasure of half drowning themselves in black mud, I don't see why I shouldn't sell a few gallons of Pure Scottish Peat Water to a few rich

Americans. You haven't seen anything yet! The next thing I am going to sell down the King's Road is cricket bat with Sober's autograph, which will help me to become a rare collector of Chelsea dolly birds, and I will screw them from dawn to sunset!

JACKIE: So you give up lying to older women for their money. I have never had any idea where you learned to be such a cheat. Any more champagne, please?

SHAKIE: Yes, the fridge is full of the stuff.

JACKIE: It'll always give me great pleasure to drink your champagne. I will compromise with you. Darling I will only drink your champagne slowly, non-stop. The same way I would like to drain your body of the fluid that give you cockstand at such an early age. I remember when my body flaw your tiny little heart all because your eyes get stuck between my legs. The little boy was totally hooked for a couple of weeks. Perhaps I would have felt better if the government had charged me with conspiracy to cause an explosion to your cock.

SHAKIE: And that's the most serious charge in England at the moment and I would have been better off murdering you a long time ago. Never mind my baby mother I have always had an atomic shelter in my heart for you.

JACKIE: Next time it will be the American and the Japanese war for us. By the way, my suitcase is still at the railway station. I haven't yet made up my mind where to stay.

SHAKIE: You can stay here if you like.

JACKIE: What? You must be joking! Stay here and allow you to rape me?

SHAKIE: Oh, piss off and shut up!

JACKIE: Don't bully me, you sex maniac.

SHAKIE: I will collect your suitcase later.

JACKIE: I hope to see some old friends while I am up here for these few precious days. Could I sleep on your settee then?

SHAKIE: You could sleep in the shit house for all I care. (*Phone rings.*)

JACKIE: What's that?

SHAKIE: What do you think?

JACKIE: I don't know, the Post Office must have gone mad to let us use their telephone for your dirty work. Well answer the bloody thing!

SHAKIE: Oh let them wait. If it is bothering you, answer it.

JACKIE: That's your phone. It could be Captain Morgan enquiring about the slave trade from Africa. Ah! The mellow and beauty of champagne makes one quite witty! I will go to the kitchen for refills. I don't wish to hear what you have to say to your tarts. Shall I cook you something to eat later?

(*As she exits to kitchen SHAKIE is speaking.*)

SHAKIE: No, I am not hungry. But help yourself to whatever you want.

JACKIE: (*Calling from kitchen.*) Thank you!

SHAKIE: (*Into phone.*) Ya! Hey! What's happening Stumpie! What, man I haven't seen you since our last orgy. When did you get back from Germany? Sorry Stumpie. I forget you only left yesterday. You remember my baby mother? Well, she's here with a load of fucking troubles. I see, you are only round the corner. Yeah, come on over. Okay see you later.

(*JACKIE enters with a glass of port.*)

JACKIE: Nice, vintage port as well! Who was it?

SHAKIE: You will find out soon enough.

JACKIE: So your freak friend turned up after all? Interesting. I remember the last time we met.

SHAKIE: Do you always have to listen through keyholes?

JACKIE: When I am with you, yes.

SHAKIE: I am going to change. If the phone rings, tell them I'm out.

JACKIE: You mean you are going to demob yourself from the army uniform? Next thing you will tell me is that you only wear the uniform to publicise your African trade with Western Europe.

SHAKIE: You're feeling real nice, eh?

(*SHAKIE exits to bedroom. JACKIE walks around the room, looking at all the furniture, examining everything. She opens*

*a drawer, finds SHAKIE's diary, begins to turn the pages.
Closes after a few pages and puts it back. She sits, very relaxed.)*

JACKIE: My God! Eighteen years of age. (*She sips her port
and sighs.*) I wonder who owns this flat? What's the matter
with me? What do I care who owns what flat. (*She looks at
her port and smiles. Exchanges port for glass of champagne.*)
Champagne should be reserved for rich old men to
celebrate wench's twenty-first birthday. I might as well
finish the bottle. (*Empties the rest of champagne bottle into
her glass.*) It's to be another mad night. I know it. He's
going to rape me. Sex, sex, sex. He's bloody sex mad!
(*Swallows half the champagne in the glass at one gulp.*)
Anyway, I think my life could be worse. At least, I am
my own boss. I choose what I do. No regrets. I am lucky.
Priscilla is a beautiful baby. I am glad she is happy.
Even on this night I shall remain flamboyant as ever.
(*She drains the glass but keeps it in her hand.*) I hope he
takes me dancing. No, that would be too much for his
blood pressure. I would eat the little bastard. No, I must
remain calm. (*Puts glass down.*)
(*SHAKIE enters, smartly dressed, Carnaby Street style. Goes
to the mirror, brushing himself, looking very pleased.*)
No wonder the fridge is full with champagne. I wouldn't
be surprised if it wasn't another old woman like myself,
with a credit card, doing such nice things for you.

SHAKIE: At 15, when I catch you on the King's Road, did I
ask you back to my place for tea? Nope. I said, 'Let's go
back to my place for coffee.' There is a vast difference
between tea and coffee. And ever since that day, you used
me as your psychiatric patient.

JACKIE: No darling, you are wrong. I was only your doctor
when we first met but I am now a qualified psychiatrist
just for you.

SHAKIE: But little do you know that Jackie Jackass is the
fucking patient.

JACKIE: Well, how can you make so much money? Not
selling water, I am sure. The trouble with you is that you
think you are the only person that can screw me.

98

SHAKIE: Come off this sex trip, you're making me sick.

JACKIE: If I need sex I have a dozen boyfriends to screw me.

SHAKIE: How old are they?

JACKIE: Men, not stupid kids.

SHAKIE: Didn't you enjoy it when I screw you at 15?

JACKIE: Once – the first time. Not when you raped me two hundred times after that.

SHAKIE: How does your boyfriend feel about you having a baby for a 15-year-old boy?

JACKIE: Nobody is interested in you. You are full of shit ego.

SHAKIE: Me and you is the last tango in Paris. I am glad I am such a wise man; if I was stupid I would be hooked on you for the rest of my life. Then, when I am 30, I would find out that your greatest love is to screw 15-year-old boys. What a rass clath waste.

JACKIE: You should be dead immediately for saying such things. You are the only 15-year-old I ever screw. God! What a mistake!

SHAKIE: Right on sister! It was also a mistake to let Sobers play in the last test match at Lords.

JACKIE: Shut up and talk sense.

SHAKIE: You spend your life living like a prostitute, desperate for emotional satisfaction out of other black people. I am sure you have always wanted to be a psychiatrist. Always searching for other people's soul and never finding your own. What's a freak like you doing working for the council and at the same time living with a retired schoolteacher! It's women like you who definitely let down black people. Sell your soul for a little comfort. I want to be a millionaire out of King's Road or Portobello Road, I don't care which road it is.

JACKIE: Tell me the truth. Is this your flat?

SHAKIE: Yes! One million times!

JACKIE: Where did you get the money?

SHAKIE: I sell the water bar to an American.

JACKIE: How much did he pay for it? Ten pounds?

SHAKIE: No. Twenty-seven thousand dollars. (*He gets bank statement from drawer.*)

Here is my bank account. Nine thousand pounds and
a few hundred.

JACKIE: Open another bottle of champagne please.

SHAKIE: Hell! You're drinking a lot tonight.

JACKIE: You don't know me. I drunk bottles of this stuff
since I was fifteen. Father is a great lover of good
French wine.

SHAKIE: What kind of a black man was he to have such
exquisite taste?

JACKIE: Not was. He is still alive. Boy, you are rough.
Really rough! I am very proud of my middle-class
background. I had a strict and pleasant upbringing. I, I am
not ashamed of being middle class. I am not jealous.
Remember we are lovers! I mean me and you little boy
blue not Daddy and I.

STUMPIE: (*Off.*) Hey! Motherfucker! Open the door before
I kick it down.

SHAKIE: Stumpie!

STUMPIE: (*Off.*) Open the door, man!

SHAKIE: It's open man.

STUMPIE: (*Off.*) Okay. (*Kicks door open and enters with a
suitcase in each hand.*)

SHAKIE: Stumpie.

(*STUMPIE drops suitcase.*)

STUMPIE: Shit! What's happening white nigger!

SHAKIE: Shit man! Look at you!

(*They hug and shake hands.*)

Man have some champagne. (*He exits to kitchen.*)

STUMPIE: Wow! What a nice-looking woman! (*Takes off
jacket and shoes, gets ready to relax.*) Howdy ma'am!

JACKIE: Piss off! I am taking no rubbish from you tonight.
I remember what happened the last time we met.

STUMPIE: Sorry, I don't remember.

JACKIE: How long have you two delinquents known each
other?

STUMPIE: Years and years ago. Since I was 13. Mind you,
Shakie was only 10 at the time!

(*SHAKIE returns with open bottle of champagne.*)

SHAKIE: I see you two know each other.

STUMPIE: Yes man, we just met. She seems to think I should remember her.

SHAKIE: Yeah man, she's my baby mother.

STUMPIE: Hell man! What? Your baby mother! She is a woman.

SHAKIE: Do you expect me to have a baby with a man?

JACKIE: (*Laughs.*) So you don't remember?

STUMPIE: Sorry, what's your name?

JACKIE: Jackie.

SHAKIE: Didn't I ever tell you about her?

STUMPIE: No man.

JACKIE: You two will always remain criminals.

SHAKIE: Hell Stumpie! Let's drink to your homecoming!

JACKIE: Yes, why not. Cheers!

(*They all touch glasses, laugh. Blackout.*)

End of Act One.

ACT TWO

When the lights come on, room is slightly untidy; empty bottles, shoes, coats, STUMPIE's silk scarf lying about. STUMPIE and SHAKIE enter, slightly drunk. They have been out on the town all night. They are deep in discussion of business.

SHAKIE: Man, I tell you music is not my scene.

STUMPIE: But man, with your influence you could help a lot of black people.

SHAKIE: Not me. There is only two kinds of people in this world; buyers and sellers. Everybody buy and sell everybody else's business.

STUMPIE: Well, then, why not buy and sell black people music. There is 300 million Africans. One hit record and you have got a million seller on your hands.

SHAKIE: Man, that is a dream. Two hundred years too late! Down at King's Road is the United Nations. They all come to the King's Road – African, Indian, Japanese, even prince and princess, they are all freaks come to King's Road to buy old cloths from Saturday to Saturday. Black musician actors including the rass claht black Americans line up like an army of studmen ready to pounce on Chelsea nightclub parties. How can you work like that? They let you down the minute they set eyes on a white mini skirt and the black women grab the first rich beatnik that come along.

STUMPIE: Man you mad to rass claht! Don't talk like that about black people. Real black people don't go to Chelsea.

SHAKIE: They look black enough for me, especially the Americans. I feel sorry for them, but I am not going to lend you five thousand pounds to give to charity.

STUMPIE: Charity? What the rass claht is this? There is plenty money involved in the deal for us.

SHAKIE: Of course it is charity! The highest level any black singer will reach in England is a twenty pound a week chorus job in a West End production. The leading

lady may be singing about black people's blues, but the
black faces always remain in the chorus line. The only
profession black people do well is the oldest profession
of them all – giving away cock and pussy for nothing.
Take me for example. When I first started selling water
down the King's Road everybody think I was mad. But
I wasn't selling water, I was selling sympathy. That's why
rich people will always do business with me, they think
I've got good intentions. White people think I will
never get further than a barman in a discotheque down
Chelsea. I watch everybody down King's Road, black
and white. They are the show piece of English middle-
class beatnik society.

STUMPIE: Hippies!

SHAKIE: No. Rass clath beatniks! The only successful
business you will be able to do with middle-class
beatniks is to sell them old clothes or African leftover
junk. Middle-class people only have enough money to
buy one cheap Christmas present at the end of the year,
for their friends. If you really want to make money, you
have to do business with rich people or poor people;
poor people have to spend all their money on food or
they will die of starvation. That's why I am going to take
a close look on how black people spend their money on
food in Portobello Road and Shepherd Bush market.
Rich people's greatest love is leisure, and that's where
they spend most of their money. I want to be a man of
leisure, so I sell big African monster chair to rich people
for two hundred and fifty pounds each, and I can't hope
for a better life. I am happy to spend the rest of my life
in Chelsea selling African chairs to the stockbrokers'
green belt in and around the home counties. Lick them
rass clath Sobers!

STUMPIE: Man, Shakie, you are talking politics and
running away from the issue.

SHAKIE: Not politics, man, facts!

STUMPIE: How can you sit there and talk about blacks.
Man, you are twice as bad as the freaks you talk about.

You can't blame black people for their downfall. At last me and a few others is trying to do something. Black people are not stupid. All we need is a little money. These are good musicians. They are not stupid.

SHAKIE: Oh yeah? Then how come they never get further than the King's Road?

STUMPIE: Who gets further than the King's Road?

SHAKIE: Black people!

STUMPIE: Those few freak black people down King's Road are dead. Man I am talking constructive business about constructive people. Look at the history of black people's music. Doesn't it make you sick?

SHAKIE: No, I like dancing to it as much as any white beatnik.

STUMPIE: Man you're talking fuckery! Leave white people's business alone and help a few black people. I have the studio, the equipment…all we need is a little money for publicity and food until we get on our feet. These people are depending on me. I can't let them down. The difference between you and me, Shakie, is that you cry with your eyes closed and I cry with mine wide open. Shakie, you're a good businessman, I admit that, but I am also a businessman. Travel Europe and Africa, I see what's happening to black people music. There is no big black bands in Europe, yet Europe is so close to Africa.

SHAKIE: That's exactly what I mean! But I bet you Europe is not short of black prostitutes, male and female. From Paris to Stockholm the black man is better known for his big prick. LICK THEM RASS CLATH SOBERS! I feel drunk. Pour me some champagne.

(*STUMPIE pours two glasses of champagne.*)

STUMPIE: It's true you talking, but I can't give up. Boy, black people really can fuck!

(*Phone rings.*)

What time is it?

SHAKIE: Five-thirty. I don't understand it. Who could be phoning me at this time in the morning? Answer it, Stumpie, it could only be my father.

STUMPIE: Man I don't want to talk to your old man.

SHAKIE: Jesus Christ what is this? I better answer it myself.
(*Picks up receiver, STUMPIE gives him champagne.*)
Yes, what is? Oh, Brian! Yeah; man, I did say you could
call me any time. Yeah, I understand. What is it? What!
I will be right over. Sorry...yeah, it's five-thirty in the
morning. Okay. seven-thirty. I will be there. How many
chairs arrive?...Ten?...What's the going price if I take
the lot?...Fifty each...I can only sell them for 55. No,
man. Knock it down to 40. I will take the lot...Okay.
I understand...cash not cheque. No, I don't have to wait
until the bank open. I will be there as soon as I feel fit
enough. Yes, I am sure. See you. (*Hangs up.*) Stumpie,
I am paying 40 pounds each for handmade African
chairs that I am selling for 250 guineas.

STUMPIE: How do you manage to do that?

SHAKIE: Well, I am in business with some carpenter up
north. Boy, I tell you I am a genius! I employ genuine
African craftsmen to work in a farmhouse up north to
make African arts and crafts. I am in the import business,
but transportation is only from Yorkshire to Chelsea. So
why should I lend you money to import 20 African
musicians? And how are you going to get them past
Mister Enoch Powell's Immigration Army when they are
not even Pakistanis? Man, you are wasting your time.
Come into business with me in Portobello Road. Yam and
sweet potato, that is your business!

STUMPIE: Stop talking shit man. I went to Africa. I have
the whole band line-up. We can't lose! Doesn't it make
you sick to see what they do to black people music on
a Saturday night on British television! I want to put
African drums on television with African faces. The
African drum will be the sound of the future, and like
a good businessman I can feel it in my bones. Don't you
see it? There is no regular black band on television.
Nowhere in public can you see black people playing
their own music. Something got to be done before it's
too late. You are one of the most fascist black men

I ever met, so why don't you help these poor African musicians? If these musicians come to England, white people will stop thieving their music and we will be a lot richer.

SHAKIE: You are not a businessman, you are a puritan dreamer! Which television channel is your African musicians going to appear on? Not these in England, I am sure of that to rass clath! Is only two kind of programmes on British television; it's either Lulu or the comedians. Well, you could say that Charlie Williams is there with them, but, on the other hand, he used to play regular Saturday football for Doncaster which again is in Yorkshire. So let's import from Yorkshire and forget about Africa. Stumpie, as soon as your friends arrive in London from Africa they will be down King's Road buying old clothes with the little money I got saved. Black people will never have a regular spot on television because white people is not going to give up their regular army of English comedians for the sake of a few Africans. When you watch English comedians on television, all they do is shape their face to take the mickey out of Harold Wilson and Ted Heath! White people sure know how to look after their own. What a fuck up situation! You should take a walk on King's Road and tell the black beatnik to stop giving away cock and pussy to white people for next to nothing. Take my old man. He was one of the greatest musicians in the West Indies. You yourself said he played the flute better than any shepherd. He drag me from the other side of the world when I was eight, and the only place he ever take me is pubs. So for seven years a week and twice on Sunday! Sundays is the day for jazz in England. You see, Stumpie, black people never get further than pubs with their music in England. Pub, pub, seven rass clath night a week, and the most money my father ever have in his pocket is one ounce of ganja and a bottle of whiskey. So leave black people music in Africa where it belong. British television will only use black people music for signature tunes on Late Night Line-Up.

STUMPIE: Shakie, if I did not know you well enough,
I would say you hate black people. Man, you painting a
black picture of black people. But I will never give up
trying. Yes sir! I am going to sit in my front room and
watch black people singing their song in their own
Saturday night spectacular on television! Shakie, it no
use you trying to change my mind. If you don't give me
the money I will only go to the Jew man and lose
everything. (*Stops and thinks.*) Jesus Christ! I am so
frustrated! Music is in my blood! I can't give up so
early in my life.

SHAKIE: Then I feel sorry for you. What you don't realise,
Stumpie, is that nothing ever change in this country.
England is a freedom country for free speech. Anybody can
go to Hyde Park Corner and talk a lot of shit, as long as
they don't try to change anything. White people will never
allow black musicians to compete against the Osmond
brothers. This is the country where 14-year-old girls fall in
love with nine-year-old pop singers! Stumpie, it's yam and
sweet potato for you in Portobello Road – or you could do
better and pack up and go to Africa where people will
appreciate black people music.

STUMPIE: Never. I will leave when all the other black
people leave. Not before to rass clath. So Mr Powell
better hurry up and become Prime Minster!

SHAKIE: Now you making sense!

STUMPIE: You want to tell me that black people is
doomed to prostitution in this country?

SHAKIE: Yes, as long as there is people like Mr Powell,
but I am glad to say Europe cannot get away from the
Chinese.

STUMPIE: That's fucking right! The Chinese have got
them. I will never give up until I do the same thing for
us blacks. There is so much soul in Africa that even the
earth is blessed! It's a pity that you never visit Africa.
If only you did, then you would see a whole continent of
people, young at heart and bursting with energy. Even
the animals are the biggest in the world!

SHAKIE: I have nothing against Africa. It's the King's
Road that's causing all the trouble. That is the road
where the beatniks walk along every morning to go and
talk shit and rubbish on radio and television.

(*JACKIE enters, jumper and trousers, no shoes.*)

JACKIE: Why do you have such a big mouth! I really can't
sleep with so much noise going on.

SHAKIE: You have a cheek, sleeping in my bed fully clothed.

JACKIE: I told you I don't trust you.

STUMPIE: Would you like a drink?

JACKIE: No thank you. Have you collected my cases?

SHAKIE: No, I am going out in a minute. I will collect
it then.

JACKIE: Jesus Christ! What a sight! Anybody for coffee?

STUMPIE: No thank you.

SHAKIE: I am strictly a champagne man.

JACKIE: Stop showing off so early in the morning. (*She sits
on settee.*)

SHAKIE: We will have to talk about this again, Stumpie.
If you did want the money to go and set up business in
Africa, that would be different.

STUMPIE: I will be glad when every black man is kicked
out of England. Until that happens, these African
musicians must come here and play their music.

SHAKIE: Listen, man, why don't you come with me to
collect the chairs?

STUMPIE: No, man. I got problems. I have got to work
this thing out.

SHAKIE: Alright, I'll see you later.

STUMPIE: That's alright. Yes, it's got to be the Jew man.

SHAKIE: They have a lot of money.

STUMPIE: I am confused. I don't want to use the Jew
man's money. Hell! I think I will go and hang about
Africa for a while.

SHAKIE: You want to come with me Jackie?

JACKIE: Come where with you? To rob the Americans?

SHAKIE: Shut up! We've been discussing serious business
all night.

JACKIE: Well, is the Bank of England safe?

SHAKIE: I told you, cut the crap!

STUMPIE: Hey, hold up, man, not first thing in the morning!

SHAKIE: Anyway, I got to go. Stumpie, don't do anything before we talk again.

STUMPIE: OK. See you later.

SHAKIE: Right, see you. (*He exits.*)

STUMPIE: Are you enjoying yourself?

JACKIE: No. Have you got a cigarette?

STUMPIE: Sure. (*He lights a cigarette for her.*) Wow! You look just as beautiful first thing in the morning! You are some woman!

JACKIE: Are you always like this?

STUMPIE: Like what?

JACKIE: Flattering. Where is that mad boy off to so early?

STUMPIE: Why do you keep referring to Shakie as if he is a boy?

JACKIE: Well, what is he?

STUMPIE: You can't live without him can you?

JACKIE: What? Don't be so damned stupid! Just because he screw me a few times? Don't make me laugh!

STUMPIE: That's not what I mean.

JACKIE: What do you mean?

STUMPIE: One thing for sure, ma'am, you're a beautiful woman.

JACKIE: Oh, stop it!

STUMPIE: Do you work?

JACKIE: Of course I work.

STUMPIE: What do you do?

JACKIE: I work for the council.

STUMPIE: Doing what?

JACKIE: Social work.

STUMPIE: Where? Camden council?

JACKIE: Yes, why?

STUMPIE: What exactly do you do for the council?

JACKIE: I work with young people. I don't want to talk about it.

STUMPIE: Now I see it!

JACKIE: See what?

STUMPIE: You see Shakie as a teenage delinquent.

JACKIE: I see him as a prize pigeon. Nevertheless, I wonder where he gets his money.

STUMPIE: You mean you don't know?

JACKIE: He promised he could take care of our baby Priscilla.

STUMPIE: Believe me, he can afford it. He is a rich man.

JACKIE: He flash me a bank statement last night for over nine thousand pounds. I don't believe it.

STUMPIE: That's nothing. Me and him together is going to make millions.

JACKIE: I am not a child. Stop trying to impress me.

STUMPIE: You are a pretty woman, but you are old-fashioned.

JACKIE: Old-fashioned, when I let a 15-year-old boy screw me? And give me a baby on top of it?

STUMPIE: That was the crossroad of your life.

JACKIE: I have always think young. I want to free myself from the claws of human beings. It is only in the young we women can find such freedom. I don't regret having the baby for Shakie. God! How I wish that boy would grow up.

STUMPIE: But he is a fully grown man. You don't see him that way, that's all.

JACKIE: I don't trust him. He is sneaky and creepy. I am not accustomed to that kind of people.

STUMPIE: What kind of people?

JACKIE: People who walk the street day and night. Non-stop.

STUMPIE: God almighty! You are fucking prejudiced as well. A right upper-class bitch.

JACKIE: You are not doing bad yourself.

STUMPIE: I am a black businessman for black people. I only talk black people business. That is how I get my money.

JACKIE: Why are you so aggressive?

STUMPIE: Because I want to.

JACKIE: Do you know I was almost in love with Shakie once?

STUMPIE: I wouldn't know. I don't like women.

JACKIE: Now I see your little game! I bet you was disappointed when you found me here last night.

STUMPIE: What?

JACKIE: You are jealous! Don't let him stop you from having a love affair with him.

STUMPIE: You kinky as well! You think we two is queer?

JACKIE: Of course you are.

STUMPIE: Shut up! You too fucking stupid. You are a disgrace to black people.

JACKIE: A right black power bastard.

STUMPIE: Black power frighten you?

JACKIE: I am a social worker.

STUMPIE: I know.

JACKIE: Black men are too barbaric. No bloody culture. Look at the Jews; at least they fight for their culture.

STUMPIE: You are a lousy Englishwoman.

JACKIE: I beg your pardon. I am blacker than you, mate!

STUMPIE: Texture of skin, yes. But you are still a fucking Englishwoman. Just imagine, the council employ an idiot like you to run poor people life. The council is not just exploiting your body, they are also using your little non-knowledge of black people history.

JACKIE: Well I got enough knowledge about black power and revolution! I am sick and tired of drop-out people. That council work was driving me mad before I went to Jamaica. Jesus Christ! Problem, problem. Everybody want everything for nothing. I had to take Priscilla home to Jamaica. At least she is happy in Jamaica. Now I am just going to stay around and enjoy myself. And whether you like it or not, I am going to live in this flat. If he man enough to give me a baby then he man enough to support me.

STUMPIE: Why are you telling me your business? I really hate you, you fascist bastard. There is no Jew living in this flat. We don't even have a Sammy Davis LP. Tell me something, where in the West Indies have you seen any Chinese, Jews, Arabs or white people who is starving?

111

And look at you, bragging about white people who run Camden council to rass clath!

JACKIE: What are you talking about?

STUMPIE: You talk about blacks as if they are shit. I don't like anybody who don't like black people.

JACKIE: Oh, my God! I have got another baby on my hands! (*She laughs.*)

STUMPIE: So you are not worried how the Jews, the Arabs and the Chinese are living in big comfortable houses in the West Indies where you just come from? And at the same time, police and soldiers surrounded the black people with machine guns. And middle-class black people like yourself do nothing except watch them die of starvation!

JACKIE: You lost me. I don't know what you are talking about. It's too early in the morning for this kind of discussion.

STUMPIE: It is never too early to talk about how white people is thieving black people's music.

JACKIE: What are you talking about this time again?

STUMPIE: You remind me of my kid brother girlfriend.

JACKIE: Oh? What's that supposed to mean?

STUMPIE: It means you need a surprise. (*He comes nearer to her.*)

JACKIE: Oh! (*Stands up.*) I am going to make some tea. Would you like a cup?

STUMPIE: (*Slaps her hard across the face.*) That's what I did to my kid brother girlfriend!
(*JACKIE, shocked and bewildered, stops, pulls herself together, sits in original seat. STUMPIE watches for her reaction.*)

JACKIE: What am I supposed to do, cry for you? Well, well. One give me a baby, the other beat me up!

STUMPIE: What you don't seem to realise is that white people believe that the only way the blacks will get what rightfully belongs to them is through evolution and not revolution. Revolution must come, starting with you! (*He slaps her hard across the face.*) If I don't get the 20 musicians from Africa then it's gonna be voodoo from

112

Haiti! Black people's music is a spiritual happening that give poor black people the extra strength and courage they need to survive in white people's country. My spirit tells me that you are no fucking good. It's no use looking at me like that unless you need another few slaps. Look woman, I am not a person – I am a character, black people's character, that's me! That's me – I am good, bad and indifferent!

JACKIE: Have you finished?

STUMPIE: How can I finish what I haven't started?

JACKIE: Why did you hit me? Can't you get it through your head that I have no idea what you are talking about? Why pick on me?

STUMPIE: I don't like middle-class black people especially those that go around fucking with white people to achieve equality.

JACKIE: (*Shouting.*) SHUT UP! (*She throws her cigarette at him.*) Bloody mad kid! Horrible bastard!

STUMPIE: What are you doing? Put out the cigarette before you burn the place down! (*He puts out the cigarette.*)

JACKIE: Why are you such a brutal beast? You are really mad!

STUMPIE: Of course I am mad when I haven't got any money!

JACKIE: What have that got to do with me?

STUMPIE: Nothing!

JACKIE: Just because your friend is my baby father, it doesn't entitle you to slap me across the face when you feel like it.

STUMPIE: I don't want to hear none of your business.
(*Walks over to the radio cassette and switches on 'In the Ghetto' by Lloyd Robinson. He starts to dance by himself.*)
Why don't you groove to the music?

JACKIE: Why, why! For God's sake! (*She rushes into the bedroom, crying.*)

STUMPIE: (*Smiling.*) So you don't want to dance?
(*STUMPIE gets a large joint from the drawer. Lights it and continues to dance and sing to the music. JACKIE comes out of the bedroom wiping her eyes and sniffing.*)

JACKIE: That's why you are so bloody brutal! You are
    nothing but a junkie! Leave me alone! I don't like people
    who slap my face. I am not afraid to blow off your
    fucking head with a shotgun!

STUMPIE: Stop shouting war woman when I am smoking
    the peace pipe.

    (*SHAKIE enters.*)

JACKIE: Oh, piss off!

SHAKIE: What's going on?

JACKIE: That bastard just slapped me twice for nothing!

SHAKIE: So you give the woman a few slaps, Stumpie?

STUMPIE: Man, I was only putting a little soul in her.

SHAKIE: Haven't she got any? Give me the ganja spliff, man.

STUMPIE: No, I don't think so. (*Hands him the joint.*)

JACKIE: Oh, God! Forgive me! (*She runs into the bedroom.*)

SHAKIE: Hey! Where are you going? You got some
    explanations to do.

JACKIE: Leave me alone the bloody lot of you! (*She slams
    bedroom door.*)

STUMPIE: Boy I feel tired to rass cloth. (*Falls flat on his
    face.*)

SHAKIE: Get up, man. You have to give me a hand with
    Jackie trunk.

STUMPIE: What trunk?

SHAKIE: Funny, all sorts of things happen to me today.
    I didn't get the chair. I waited for a while, but he
    didn't turn up.

STUMPIE: Where were you suppose to meet him?

SHAKIE: The antique market.

STUMPIE: What! At this time in the morning?

SHAKIE: I wonder what happened to him? Man, I make a
    lot of money out of those chairs.

STUMPIE: Yes I know. You told me.

SHAKIE: I will have to go and look for him in a minute.

STUMPIE: What were you saying about Jackie's trunk?

SHAKIE: Has she told you anything? (*Pointing at bedroom.*)

STUMPIE: Like what?

SHAKIE: Like where she's coming from. Did she say
    anything about the baby? Or Jamaica?

STUMPIE: Yes, I think she said the baby's in Jamaica with her father, and that she give up working for the council.

SHAKIE: Boy, that woman is a born liar! She frighten me to rass cloth. I think she come back to take over my life.

STUMPIE: What do you mean?

SHAKIE: Well, she told me she was living down south with a retired Jewish schoolteacher. It's all lies! She just come back from Jamaica!

STUMPIE: No, man, she works for Camden council.

SHAKIE: I just collect them from Victoria Station.

STUMPIE: Victoria Railway Station? But you just said she came back from Jamaica yesterday.

SHAKIE: That's what I can't understand.

STUMPIE: So how did you know she only came back from Jamaica yesterday?

SHAKIE: The label on her trunk.

STUMPIE: Ah! Now I see it! That's why she's so sceptical. Man, is come the woman come to live with you! Somebody must have told her that you are doing well! So she come back to collect a few fur coats!

SHAKIE: No, man. She's rich! She don't want my money.

STUMPIE: (*Very excited. Stands up quickly.*) What? She's rich! Come on, let's get her trunk in! I must apologise to her immediately! Boy, I really sorry I hit her.

SHAKIE: By the way, why did you hit her?

STUMPIE: Never mind about that! Come on, let's get her trunks from the van.

SHAKIE: Hold it, man. What's the fuck wrong with you? This is serious.

STUMPIE: What is serious about rich people? If she is rich, then you must love her. You don't have to be serious, I love every rich woman. I never did care whether they were black or white. The only nation of cock that doesn't have a religion is the black man cock. The black man joined every religion across the globe only to fuck their women.

SHAKIE: The woman is 30, I am 18. I can't manage her.

STUMPIE: Well, give her to me. I can look after her. Man, there is 20 African musicians waiting to come to England!

SHAKIE: Forget about your stupid dream. She won't give you a penny. I am worried about Bryan and those chairs. I wonder if anything gone wrong? I got quite a few customers waiting for those chairs. Did my old man phone while I was out?

STUMPIE: No.

SHAKIE: I wonder what happen to him?

STUMPIE: Are you going to live with the woman?

SHAKIE: I don't know. Let's get the luggage and leave her alone, after all, she is my baby mother.

STUMPIE: Sure, Okay. You are a good businessman, but you don't understand women.

SHAKIE: Lay off, Stumpie. I am worried about a few things.

STUMPIE: Okay. Let's get her luggage.

(*Black out.*)

End of Act Two.

ACT THREE

JACKIE is dressed in black, head bowed, leaning against the wall.
STUMPIE is sitting on the floor, smoking a big joint, with 'Melody
Maker' in front of him on the floor. SHAKIE is sitting on a chair,
head between his knees. STUMPIE walks along to SHAKIE, gives
him the joint. SHAKIE inhales deeply, coughs, then hands STUMPIE
the joint. STUMPIE refuses, shaking his head.

STUMPIE: Smoke man!
    (*SHAKIE sits back, relaxed, ready to enjoy the joint.*
    STUMPIE picks up 'Melody Maker', slowly walking round
    the room, reading to himself.)

JACKIE: He was your father.

SHAKIE: Let the dead bury their dead.

JACKIE: Look, I already paid for the car to take us to
    Manchester. It's only his funeral – that's the least you can
    do for him. How can you refuse to go to your own
    father's funeral?

STUMPIE: He died in the gutter like a dog.

JACKIE: Will you bloody sit down and stop pacing up and
    down the room!
    (*STUMPIE looks at her relaxed, sits on the floor.*)
    Why, why, for heaven's sake? Surely you are man
    enough to know that you have to go to your own father's
    funeral! You said yourself that he visit you every week or
    phone you to let you know what he was doing. He was a
    good man. He gave pleasure to a lot of people, and the
    first thing you did when you read in the 'Melody Maker'
    that he was dead is burn the tapes with his music, and
    make silly excuses that you don't want any beatnik
    antique dealer to get their hands on his music.

STUMPIE: He is right, because if they were going to use his
    music for the benefit of black people, it wouldn't be too
    bad. But it's some of them wicked rass clath people who
    call themselves art collectors when they are really antique
    dealers waiting for black people to drop dead so they can
    make millions out of the dead black people music.

SHAKIE: That's why all the famous blacks are dead.

STUMPIE: What do you expect when they just shoot and kill 11 of us in South Africa this year 1973!

JACKIE: Shakie, for God's sake, Manchester is where your only relation, your father, is lying in the morgue, and is going to be buried at four-thirty this afternoon. Are you going to get ready? We must hurry, there isn't much time.

SHAKIE: You are a real dreamer: There'd be a little more peace if you'd only shut up. You are wasting your time, I am not going to any funeral.

STUMPIE: Jesus Christ! Listen what they write about the man! (*Reading from newspaper.*) 'Shakie King, the well-known West Indian flute player, with his oriental-style playing, was found dead on Tuesday outside a betting shop near the Piccadilly area in Manchester. Shakie King was well known for his happy flute playing in the London pubs and around the country. No one knows for sure how he died, but he was well known for his heavy drinking. He occasionally found it difficult to breathe since he suffered from asthma. The Earl of Bullocks Sanford, who is the landlord of one of London's most famous pubs, The Cow and Two Horns, in the East End, said yesterday: "Shakie King, 'Hawk' as he is known to his friends, brought a ray of sunshine from the West Indies with his happy music." The Earl, who is the nephew of General Jestal, the famous desert fighter, ranked next to no other than Lawrence of Arabia. The Earl also has a once-famous aunt who was the first English lady to bring clean jazz to London in the late twenties and early thirties. Over the last five years the Earl says he spent the winter season skiing in Switzerland. We were interrupted from behind the bar by a buxom barmaid shouting "Nick!" It was Lady Bullocks Sanford, of course, telling Earl Bullocks Sanford that it was time for him to get weaving behind the bar. Nick went on to say how much he missed Shakie King's music. "Shakie King," he said, "was one of the last oriental great black musicians." One customer interrupted and said, "There

will be a few sad faces tonight!" Earl Bullocks Sanford
went behind the bar, kissed Lady Bullocks Sanford on
the left cheek (since she is suffering from toothache on
her right cheek) and thanked her for being so patient. He
said that the light will be dim in their hearts tonight for
Shakie King, or "Hawk", the name he will he
remembered by in the East End.'

SHAKIE: He gets a big write-up in his epitaph.

STUMPIE: It's not him they are talking about! They only
mention his name a few times. They haven't said anything
about his music.

SHAKIE: I can remember when every white man have him
believing that he was the greatest black musician in
England.

JACKIE: Well, he was! I heard him a few times in one of
those pubs down Chelsea.

SHAKIE: It's the Chelsea beatnik set kill him with cocaine.
Since he came to England he became more stupid
every day.

JACKIE: What are you talking about? You refuse to go to
his funeral – your own father – Priscilla's grandfather!
What will you tell your daughter? Your father died and
you refused to go to his funeral! Maybe you are a kid or
a man. I don't know, but pay a little respect. See your
father on his last journey to his grave. How can you
lose? He was your father who I know loved you very
much.

SHAKIE: Amen! Stumpie, light up another Fidel-Castro
Havanna-type ganja spliff. I should be out on the street
beating the bass drum! And let the dead bury their dead.
Because John saw them coming to rass cloth.

JACKIE: Which John?

STUMPIE: John de Baptist inside the Bible saw them
coming robe in white!

JACKIE: And if John the Baptist was here today, he would
tell Shakie to go to Manchester where his father is lying
dead waiting to be buried! Oh, God! He must have died
a lonely man! If the dead could speak he would kill you

two bastards for the little sanity that's left in this world!
Why don't you go to your father funeral? Or, if you
don't want to go with me, take Stumpie. It's only four
days ago he was here talking to the both of you. Don't
you care to find out how he died?

SHAKIE: Can the dead speak the English language?

STUMPIE: Not even the live black man can speak English
alphabetical language. For five hundred years Europe has
been teaching the black man their different English
languages; and to this day the black man is not advanced
enough to spell his name in the white people language.

SHAKIE: How can they learn to spell their names when they
don't even know which tribe in Africa they belong to?

STUMPIE: The only name the blacks got in white people
language is ghetto and jungle to rass cloth!

SHAKIE: And not even jungle will last, because the white
man will soon turn every woodland in the West Indies
into supermarket.

STUMPIE: I suppose they would like to keep Africa as
their big hypermarket centre.

SHAKIE: Not a rass cloth chance. Because John saw them
coming – white robe and white faces!

JACKIE: Your father is dead in Manchester. Dead! This is
the last chance you will have to see his face before they
bury him.

STUMPIE: Bury him? You mean burn him! There is no
ground space left to bury poor people in England. That's
one of the reasons Mr Powell wants to get black people
out of England – they are short of burial space and the
good book say that ten thousand of us shall fall.

JACKIE: More like ten billion if all the other bastards is
like you two.

SHAKIE: Rass cloth! The old man dead!

STUMPIE: And it shall be that every soul shall not
hearken to that prophet from among the people.
Acts 3, verse 22.

JACKIE: Bloody acting bastard. Why don't you do
something? At least you can go to Manchester to collect
his flute and belongings from the morgue.

STUMPIE: What flute? It's a fife made out of bamboo. That was the instrument he played.

SHAKIE: What belongings did he have – a quarter-bottle of whiskey and some hash...

STUMPIE: Which is not even good ganja.

JACKIE: Jesus Christ: Jesus Christ! (*Slowly collapsing on the floor.*) God have mercy! (*She starts crying with her face in her hands.*) It's wickedness! Bloody wicked world! Wicked bastard! God! Why are they so wicked!

STUMPIE: But Peter said; 'Silver and gold have I none; but what I have, that I give thee. In the name of Jesus Christ of Nazareth, walk.' Acts 3, verse six!

(*Phone rings. SHAKIE picks up receiver and speaks into it.*)

SHAKIE: Yeah. It's alright man. I have my share of bad news for this century. Any news now is good news! What? You are joking. When? Two days ago...that's why Bryan wasn't at the market the other morning! Man, it cannot be...they are not even Pakistanis! All nine of them? Can't we do something?...Yeah, I know, no more African chairs, eh? Thanks. 'Bye. (*Hangs up. Thinks.*)

STUMPIE: What happen?

SHAKIE: It's alright. Just a minute. What a fuck up way he dial – Hello, can I speak to Mr. James Rander? Mr Shark. Yes, Shark, as in the sea. No, I don't have sharp teeth. Only when I have to bite little girls' bottom. Yes, I am young at heart, but big in the right places! Especially at bedtime with little girls like yourself! No, I am not big headed. That's what most of my women friends tell me. I can screw girls once and turn them into women. Where abouts do you live? St John's Wood – naughty, naughty! I think I will have to spank you with my little plastic belt!

(*STUMPIE exits to bedroom.*)

Yes, I like dancing before or after. What time do you finish? Four thirty? No I would rather take you to the opera. No I don't like cowboys. Thanks. I love you. Your place or mine? No we will talk about it later. You are making me impatient. I can't wait.

(*STUMPIE enters slowly, silently reading the Bible.*)

Tell me, do you know how many of the African chairs
Mr Rander have in his house? Fourteen? You sure about
that? Fourteen? Is he kinky? No...Oh I see...No I don't
want to talk to him. My beautiful darling, what colour is
your hair? Brown? Then you are deadly at nights. My
arms are waiting. You were saying that Mr Rander is not
kinky he only collect African relics. Do you know if he
ever sell any of the chairs I sell him? Oh, he also buy
and sell antiques? Tell me, how much does he sell the
king-size African chairs for? Over a thousand pounds?
No, I am sure I don't want to talk to Mr Rander. Where
do you have lunch? Suddenly a great urge come over me
to buy you lunch. No don't bother to tell him to call,
because I trust you and love you. I bet you are one of
Chelsea sexy bird. WHOOPEE I love you. What's your
favourite colour? Red? Red? Dangerous. Red rose from
me to you. Yes, I feel very spiritual today. What sign was
I born under darling? That is a secret until our first kiss.

STUMPIE: Don't matter what business a black man do in
Europe. He have to sell his cock with the business.

JACKIE: God! You are so vile and wicked, wicked, wicked,
the both of you!

STUMPIE: Just a minute. (*Puts hand over phone.*) Shut up.
I am talking on the telephone.

(*JACKIE stands up and pulls herself together.*)

JACKIE: I shall go to your father's funeral.

SHAKIE: God damn it! Who is stopping you?

(*JACKIE looks at him, then exits to the bedroom.*)

STUMPIE: You are doing overtime today.

SHAKIE: Yes man, this is a hard case. Yes, my darling.
I miss you. No, somebody was at the door darling. I am
not that lucky. I think I will buy you a boat so we could
go sailing. What sign are you? Gemini? Thank God for
that. I thought for a moment you was Taurus. That's why
I was so worried. Since we have so much in common.
Darling I've got a little problem and I trust you to solve
it for me. Mr Rander did pay me 500 pounds in advance
on another 20 king-size African chairs. Do you know

anything about it. Oh, I see. You are his wife. Why didn't you say so in the first place? How old you said you was? Sorry. I don't mind telling you my age. You are 24. I am 26. Just the right age for you. You thought I was younger? I only speak young. That's all. I will become your baby and you can mother me. (*Puts his hand over receiver.*) Stumpie, boy, this could be one of the big deals I have been waiting for. She talk like a parrot and she love sex!

STUMPIE: Good luck.

SHAKIE: I need it. Mrs Rander. Okay. Sheila.

(*JACKIE enters, mink coat, mink hat, long black gloves, diamond bracelet. Stands looking at SHAKIE. SHAKIE looks at JACKIE while talking on the phone.*)

Well, my darling, since we are going to have dinner at your place later, we really should save our energy. So my darling, your thought of the day 'Romeo is coming' see you later. 'Bye. You pretty vulture! (*Hangs up.*)

(*Looking at JACKIE.*) So you are going to the old man's funeral? Well, the rich always bury the poor.

STUMPIE: 'Ye who received the law as it was ordained by the angel, and kept it not.'

SHAKIE: Acts 3, verse 23.

STUMPIE: 'But ye who deny the Holy and the righteous one and ask for a murderer to be granted unto you.' Acts 3, verse 23.

(*JACKIE looks from STUMPIE to SHAKIE and exits quickly.*)

Are you going to get your old man a reef?

SHAKIE: The only kind of flowers my old man like is the ganja flower. I wonder what she's like? I have never noticed her when I visit Mr Rander's office.

STUMPIE: You mean the man wife that you just finished talking to on the phone?

SHAKIE: Yeah, man! I am going to screw her and count my earnings daily with my Adler adding machine.

STUMPIE: Then after a couple of weeks, when you finish with her she will write to one of those personalities like Paula, they have writing for the daily newspaper.

She will write: 'Dear Paula, I am married and got
involved with another man and in brackets – he is
coloured. Now I realise how stupid I was. I have tried to
finish the relationship more than once, but he continues
to wait outside our house until my husband leaves for
work. Then he follows me into the bedroom. I am
confused and don't know what to do. Please help!'

SHAKIE: Imagine, her husband sell the chair that I sell
him for 250 pounds for a thousand pounds or more.
(*He leaps to his feet, hand to his head, and collapses into chair.*)
Jesus, Jesus, Jesus Christ!

STUMPIE: Hell, man. Have she got that much money?

SHAKIE: Oh, God, Stumpie. No man rass cloth. This day is
too much.

STUMPIE: Sorry man. I understand about your old man.
And it's a big decision for you not to go to his funeral.

SHAKIE: No man. The dead must bury the dead. I don't
know what I can do except to rob Mr James Rander.

STUMPIE: Well, that shouldn't be hard. Man, his wife is
going to help you.

SHAKIE: I am not going to waste my money on any rass
Lily-white flower. Man, you know what they have done?
The immigration authority paid the African factory up
north and have 10 African carpenters in chains at
London Heathrow airport, ready for the first flight back
to Nigeria. Deportation to rass cloth! When they are not
even Pakistani!

STUMPIE: This time nobody can blame the police,
Mr Powell, immigration, immigration!

SHAKIE: Read me Jeremiah 27, 10 to 13.

STUMPIE: I don't have to read it, man, I know it: 'For they
prophesy a lie unto you, to remove you far from your land;
and that I should drive you out and ye should perish.'

SHAKIE: From now on my name is Jeremiah. Jeremiah
calling, and now I got to sink as low as to become a thief,
my father just drop dead in one of Manchester gutters.

STUMPIE: You see man, if you was in the music business,
you would get so much soul from it, I mean, with all

your 10 African carpenters that get deported. If they were musicians they would have left so much African drumming on tape to last you a lifetime, and make us rich for life with soulful black music.

SHAKIE: Yes, yes. I can feel my bones at my belly bottom. Jeremiah calling! Give up the King's Road! Give up women!

STUMPIE: Holy father, you are buzzing on high ground, brother. Jeremiah, let's light up the ganja peace pipe.
(*SHAKIE gets two big joints from the drawer, and gives one to STUMPIE.*)

SHAKIE: Yes, Jeremiah calling. My old man's dead. Stumpie, I am not going to bother worry myself over Mr and Mrs Rander king size African chairs from up Yorkshire. I am going to stay home and think like Fidel Castro.

STUMPIE: Wise decision. And fuck the European system the same way Castro fuck up America. This could be the right time for you to meditate and put your mind on higher ground. Promote black people music. Man, 10 percent of the people of the United States of America is slave from Africa. Man think. If we have one hit record, we could be millionaires! Forget about King's Road and England and let's go international!

SHAKIE: You really seem to have your mind set on the music scene.

STUMPIE: Let me explain to you about my African drummers. They come from a tribe of pigmy family playing together. Long before men climb down from the African trees to live on the ground. Black people can only understand one language: the drum from the Holy Mother Africa. Don't matter how many different kind of English language the white man teach the black man. Yes, sir! Black people will never understand anything unless you talk to them with the drum. The same way the white man use drums to drum out the black people out of the Gold Coast and the rest of Africa, and destroy our king and queen. Princess Ann is getting married to Captain Mark Phillips in style quite soon. The calling of

the African drum put the black people on ship out of
Africa to build big houses made out of Bath stone in
Clifton, Bristol. Yes, sir! Drum the black people out of
the deep south and into aeroplane and banana boat back
to Africa!

SHAKIE: I think I better stop grunting and groaning and
do something like drumming the black people out of the
King's Road, and bankrupt the lesbian scene. Yes, man,
drum them out of the London underground. Drum them
out of the National Assistance Boards. Drum them out of
the hospital, the prison and the mad house!

STUMPIE: Now you talking, Jeremiah! But Mr Powell don't
see it that way. Shakie, if you come in business with me,
while you are busy selling the pygmies' music, I will be
busy up and down the country supporting Mr Powell and
every Monday Club.

SHAKIE: You would have to spend a lot of time in the
Midlands. Yes, drum the black people off the buses, so
they will only have the Pakistani in Bradford saying
'Any more fares please!'

STUMPIE: Yes, brother, your name is Jeremiah! Let's work
together. The black man must take the chains off his feet
that keep him in love with beatniks.

SHAKIE: From now on, my favourite word is the drummers.

STUMPIE: Man, you are talking like a prophet!

SHAKIE: I give up the King's Road and I will take to the
Portobello Road.

STUMPIE: We might even make it to Shepherds Bush Market.

SHAKIE: I might as well become interested in politics, just
like the international beatniks down King's Road.

STUMPIE: That is a good policy. And then you could
pretend that you don't know nothing about General Amin.

SHAKIE: And stop the blood cloth beatniks from making
all the money out of black people music.

STUMPIE: And don't forget, the Jews is neck and neck with
the beatniks, pretending that they are lefties, while they
collect from the right to buy Rolls Royce. While other
white people is building us another Krupp family like the

one Hitler had in Germany building war equipment.
And since Jews and blacks are the two kind of people they
shoot down in great numbers. What is going to be at the
end of it all.

SHAKIE: And Hitler was only taking care of his own white
people in Europe by killing off the Jews. What is going
to happen to us young blacks.

STUMPIE: And everybody knows that it will be us blacks
next! So let's drum black people out of white people
prisons and into Africa.

SHAKIE: Anywhere in the world where white people drink
a lot of beer, play cricket and rugby, that's where black
people suffer the most. LICK THEM BOMB CLATH
SOBERS!

STUMPIE: South Africa is a good example. After a cricket
match and a few beers at the bar with the boys they just
go out on the street and shoot down black people.

SHAKIE: Jesus Christ! White people is really wicked! They
take the chains off the black man's neck and feet, and set
him free only to die of starvation. Black Africans have to
wait for evolution in the fifth dimension before he can
stop his children from dying of starvation while white
people continue to buy old clothes down King's Road
with gold from South Africa. There is a silver beaten into
plates brought from Tarshish, and gold from Uphaz, the
work of the artifice cunning man. This is converting time.
Take off the wool clothing. The old man is dead. The
Africans get deported. What to do? A man needs the spirit
of Africa to take him through hard times like these.
Stumpie, are you really serious about the twenty pygmies?

STUMPIE: Like you don't understand! For the last year
I done nothing but set up deals and hustle money to visit
the pygmies. Man, I am very serious. And we will make
a lot of money and at the same time, drumming black
people out of the political sex scandal which white
people choose to have so often in Europe.

SHAKIE: I hustle and have nine thousand in the bank. As
spiritual as I feel towards Africa, I still aint aim to throw
it away.

STUMPIE: It seems to me that you spend too much time down the King's Road with drop-out beatniks. You don't know the value of money. Nine thousand pounds is nothing! Don't you see how many teenage beatniks walking around the streets, flashing Barclaycards with thousands of pounds, while their mum and dad sit at home waiting for telephone calls and send them more money just in case the bank close early that day.

SHAKIE: And all the beatniks do with the money is buy old clothes and cocaine, and give black people little or nothing for their sex orgies. Stumpie, I want to come in with you, but I don't understand politics. Hustling is my business.

STUMPIE: Man, pull yourself together! How can it be politics when you are only helping black people to get what rightfully belongs to them?

SHAKIE: I tell you, as soon as the pygmies set foot in England, and drum the first note, white people will thief their music, and your pygmies will end up drumming in pubs like my father, and become a burden to the precious National Assistance Board, and fill up Dr Barnado's homes with their black bastard English children!

STUMPIE: That's why we need the pygmies in England to drum the young blacks back to Africa and cancel the Commonwealth Games.

SHAKIE: Rass clath, Stumpie. You declare war on white people.

STUMPIE: And never ending, me and you will travel black countries and tell the blacks to keep away from Europe and go back to Africa, and getting rich at the same time!

SHAKIE: I know what you mean. Sometimes I feel like breaking every law European white people ever made, just to make money. Man, they sure teach you how to go out and kill some of them before you can get any money. Revolution in England to rass clath! I feel the spirit of Jeremiah calling.

STUMPIE: Not by revolution in England, my friend. The Americans wouldn't allow it! We have to do it with the drums of the pygmies.

SHAKIE: That's what you think. You want to go two miles north of Darlington and tell the miners that there will be no revolution. I am not sure if the miners are not thinking of nationalising the White House and Buckingham Palace and put President Nixon and the Queen with the rest of the royal family on the 10 to six shift down the coal mines.

STUMPIE: I don't care pussy clath what happens to white people. They have been looking after themselves out of black people for a hundred years or more, and if they have their own way, they will continue to rob the blacks until revolution comes.

SHAKIE: Boy I feel sad because I grow up in England.

STUMPIE: Don't tell me. Go and convince white people that you are an Englishman, and see how quick the South African security force visit you.

SHAKIE: Have you worked out any practical way or schedule for the pygmies?

STUMPIE: Yeah, I have a few bookings in Germany, and a few friends is helping me in London. We figure the council might help us.

SHAKIE: Don't depend on the council for anything. That's why nearly all the black people in London with any talent have to become queer or lesbian. The only help the council give black people for their art is an old church hall in Brixton called the Dark and Light Theatre, and another one at King's Cross called the Keskidee. That's why black people are white people. Never go and watch black people work of art. The buildings are so old that if the draught don't kill you, the building will collapse and kill you instead! Stumpie! I am with you! Nine thousand plus the flat.

STUMPIE: My brother!

(*They hug each other.*)

SHAKIE: Right on! We got work to do!

STUMPIE: We will cut a double album as soon as the pygmies get here.

SHAKIE: No, no. None of that. No records.

STUMPIE: What do you mean, no records?

SHAKIE: I mean we are not going to cut any records because its white people who control the hit parade.

STUMPIE: Then how are we going to get publicity if we don't use white people media?

SHAKIE: No, we must have direct control over everything.

STUMPIE: You mean they are only going to perform for the local black community?

SHAKIE: Yes. And what a local community it's going to be!

STUMPIE: Let me in on the secret, man, and tell me how we are going to get rich out of local black people.

SHAKIE: Shit! I must get my head together. Jeremiah calling! I must get together with a few of my Jew friends.

STUMPIE: The Jew man? The deal is off. I am out! No rass clath Jew is going to run my life!

SHAKIE: Stop being so emotional. We need a lot of money for what I got in mind.

STUMPIE: Whatever it is, we don't need the Jews!

SHAKIE: Oh yes we do! I got a little Jew in me as well. Stumpie, we are going to put on one of the biggest multi-million black show this country ever seen! Right in the street of Notting Hill Gate and Ladbroke Grove festival!

STUMPIE: So how come we need white people money?

SHAKIE: The Jews are not white people.

STUMPIE: Then what are they?

SHAKIE: I don't know, but they are not white. We need the Jew man money to promote the festival.

STUMPIE: I don't follow you. man. Am I to bring the pygmies here to mash up the television set on all three channels and drum out the black people back into Africa? I don't have time for free pop show. Jimmy Hendrix play in every pop festival there is. Count Basie and Duke Ellington still performing at the royal performances at the London Palladium. Bessie Smith bleed to death reaching out to white people. Your own father drop dead in some Manchester gutter, and still white people continue to thief black people soul and music. As soon as you let white people anywhere near black people music they will thief it

and call it black rock opera, and have their own white
people doing the performances instead of the pygmies.
And now you telling me that the Jew is not white people.
It seems to me that you don't listen to General Amin. He
is better than Enoch Powell any day.

SHAKIE: Shut up man! Forget about General Amin. We
can't afford his politics. We are just two liberal young
executive from Chelsea. The first thing that you have to
straighten out, Stumpie, being involved with business
people, is your soul and emotion. You have a little too
much of both.

STUMPIE: What! I haven't got enough!

SHAKIE: Shut up man and let's plan this thing. You better
go and get pad and paper since you now become my
permanent secretary.

STUMPIE: You getting kinky!

SHAKIE: Get the rass paper, man!

STUMPIE: Okay. Jeremiah.

SHAKIE: Right, let's have some basic rules. Forget about the
pen and paper for a while. From now on, you will drive
the van. Some time today, get a big ledger book, and
don't interrupt me for the next half-hour. We need a
publicity man. I suggest we get one of the black American
freaks from off the King's Road.

STUMPIE: Suppose he's queer?

SHAKIE: Shut up, Stumpie man, I am thinking. Or, better
still, we get Jackie to do it. So much for labour force at
the moment. Now we come to money.

STUMPIE: Hold it, man! Stop! Fuck you! When it comes
to money, I am not dealing with the Jews!

SHAKIE: So, you're a coward! You are afraid of people who
are not even white!

STUMPIE: You never stop talking about how the Jews have
black men working for them for next to nothing, and at
the same time, screwing the black chicks in the back of
their Rolls Royce.

SHAKIE: That was before I planned to promote the Notting
Hill Gate annual festival. Nobody's going to rob anything.

Do you want me to go ahead with the festival without
your pygmies?

STUMPIE: No, Shakie, man. We need your help.

SHAKIE: Okay. You don't realise that the best actor among
white people is the bank manager and the champion
bank manager is a Jew man. And I aim to become a
bank manager and create a revolution inside European
monetary system.

STUMPIE: Now you're talking. Yes, we need the Jew man,
with that kind of money in mind. Jackie should do our
publicity for us. With her knowledge of cock and pussy
we should be able to extend this festival to Russia. So we
will be in Leningrad before the first batch of black
brothers gets sent down the salt mines of Siberia.

SHAKIE: LICK THEM RASS CLATH SOBERS! And
we'll have our man in Peking, voting for our pygmies.

STUMPIE: We will do it even if we have to export one of
their own Chinese in Gerrard Street in Soho. Acts of the
Romans. Chapter one.

SHAKIE: A tired man. Since the old man died, I haven't
slept.

STUMPIE: Alright, you go and get some rest. I'll go out
and get a typewriter.

SHAKIE: Good idea. Boy, there is no rest for the black
man, rush, rush, rush, all the fucking time.

STUMPIE: That's why we are the fastest runners. (*He exits.*)
(*Blackout.*)

End of Act Three.

ACT FOUR

Two weeks later, JACKIE is in nightdress, drinking fruit juice, smoking cigarette, walking about the room, very tired. STUMPIE, smartly dressed, leaning against wall, with Bible, looking fresh from a good night's sleep. SHAKIE, smartly dressed, sitting in a reclining chair, smoking big cigar, looking through a Sotheby's catalogue, looking good from a good night's sleep.

STUMPIE: The truth is the truth, no matter which way you
    look at it.

SHAKIE: Very true, Stumpie!

JACKIE: What day is it?

SHAKIE: You used to spend all your time asking what time
    is it. Now you are asking what day is it. I thought I tell
    you to put some smart clothes on.

STUMPIE: Yes, and wear some of those pretty jewels that
    you wear to the funeral. We want a good price for you.

SHAKIE: Tell it like it is, Stumpie! The days of sufferation
    is in the past.

JACKIE: Your future is blassed with syphilis. Your father
    died of syphilis in the gutter of Manchester.
    (*STUMPIE exits to kitchen.*)
    The seed of the father shall follow the children.

SHAKIE: Not me. I have one of the best specialists in
    Harley Street. And I am quite willing to make regular
    trips to the local VD clinic.

JACKIE: Syphilis shall kill you! Why are you so wicked?
    For two weeks you lock me up in this place and leave
    your henchman to watch me. Priscilla will have to
    stay a million miles away from you. No disease for my
    daughter: You will never see her again. When you're not
    raping me, your henchman is beating me up! How many
    times did I tell you that I am tired of you fucking me!
    Why don't you leave me alone.

SHAKIE: What else can I do? There's no other woman in
    the house. I have to screw somebody. And me and

Stumpie's no queer. You had your chance to leave us in
peace. Instead you hang around for the free show.

JACKIE: Some day God is going to catch up with you.
Imagine, your father die of syphilis in Manchester!
You didn't even go to his funeral.

SHAKIE: That's not the way I see it. The man who died in
the gutter of Manchester was the death of a black man,
and thousands of black people die every day with gun,
bullet and syphilis. And they are still dying off in Africa
with leprosy and starvation. I alone, with my humble self
in Chelsea cannot attend all the funerals. I am afraid the
death of one black man in Manchester doesn't move me.
The kind of funeral that I like to attend is those that they
have in Mozambique, Angola and South Africa. Good
black people funeral in 1973 is when the Portugese
massacre four hundred Africans. Right now I am waiting
for Vorster to shoot down say a round figure of a
thousand.

JACKIE: I am not your girlfriend any more. You put a stop
to all that when you lied to me about your age. Oh, my
God! My poor little Priscilla, follower of syphilis for a
father. Who is destined to be overwork nigger
Englishman, and have the audacity to call me a
middle-class bitch, and giving me orders from daybreak
to daybreak. Once and for all, when am I going to leave
this place? My trunk is packed and ready to move out of
your life. My drawers haven't been washed for a week
since I haven't changed the red pair I put on last week.
The red pair of knickers I am wearing is a defence
against you, a red guard defence, stopping you from
raping me. Baby boy, I am giving you the push and you
don't like it! Little boy blue go put on your army
uniform and let me go home to Priscilla. This mad idea
of yours is just simply fuckeries. I am not giving you a
penny of me money to put you in the Ladbroke Grove
festival. It is not my fault if you try to rob every bank
manager in London, including your rich Jew friends and
lost your nine thousand pounds. I always knew you
would die in the gutter, penniless. After all, a little boy

like you have no right to have nine thousand pounds in the first place. What are you proposing to do with me?

STUMPIE: (*Standing at door with open bottle of champagne.*) I will answer that. Sell you! Yes, madam, we are going to sell you! Maybe to the richest Jew who visit the King's Road, we don't know yet. As you know, we failed in our business venture. I cannot have my pygmies playing their music here in England. Shakie cannot promote the festival. Shakie and myself is prepared to give you the life you have always wanted. By selling you to a rich Chelsea freak, it will lift you out of your middle class society and put you in a rich society. What could be more fitting for a pretty lady like you? So let we drink the champagne and go and unlock your trunk and get ready for the King's Road!

JACKIE: Little boys, I have left you intellectually a long time ago. Sell me? You can't even sell your own assholes! You know what you can do with your champagne.

STUMPIE: Yes. Drink it! (*He pours two glasses of champagne and gives one to SHAKIE.*)

Let us drink, my friend Shakie!

SHAKIE: Certainly.

JACKIE: Pleasureful bastards! I am not your woman!

SHAKIE: When were you ever my woman? Positive thinking is positive thinking. Imagine, I spend a month of my life living with you when I was 15! Those were the days, when I take you back to my place for coffee! And you fell in love with my little one room in some attic near Bayswater. That night we slept and made love so beautifully. Next morning you make me breakfast. You then boil my eggs to suit my taste. Three days you stay with me in my attic. I was your little prince. And you make me believe you was my rich queen. You said, let's go back to your place, it is a little more comfortable at home. I did not answer. We just went cruising along in your 1972 Triumph sports car. We spend a week in bed, living and love-making. Like a lamb going to his slaughter, I kissed and caressed every part of your body.

Then you feed me with high-class Chinese food. You made several phone calls to your best friends and mentioned my name in every sentence. I was home and dry. That was the life for me! Come the third week when you nearly kill me with your erotic love-making, things began to change. You tell me that you were no money-lender. You sit up in bed all day and make no more breakfast, and said that there was more to life than sex. You complain that your middle-class background make you need intellectual stimulation. What was I to do? I am no intellectual. My heart beat so fast I had instant fever. What pain! All because I smell the sweet success of life through your beautiful eyes. You gave me 200 pounds. I get well again and buy some new clothes. You wish me luck and throw me out. I go home and just die in my bed. I arise from the dead, a new man. Pain struck me again, when I entered the King's Road from Sloane Square and see you shopping with your handsome prince – which was an African who you tell me you didn't like and you would never screw him. He was one of your friends you used to talk to on your gold-handled telephone when I was laying in your bed with you. Since that day, every time I screw you I feel guilty. My wick is not 30 inches! So all I've got to offer you is me wood, or sell you down the King's Road.

STUMPIE: Brother, what this woman done to you is the same thing white women done to the age group of your father! Having 10 black men fighting and chopping up one another over one white woman. We are not our fathers! We taste the life of the middle class when we are young. Shakie did not wait on his father to die in the gutter of Manchester before he get smart and buy himself a flat in Chelsea. Blessed are those who wait patiently! And the same flat becomes your prison for our benefit. Men like me and Shakie is like wolf in sheep's clothing. We plan to make money from our best asset, and kill two birds with one stone. By simply selling you and pension you off in some big house in the country, and make room for some other black woman.

SHAKIE: And we will sell the next black woman that takes your place down the King's Road! Young blacks like us have to learn from experienced black women like you. Over the few years I know you, you make it quite clear how rich old men love you.

JACKIE: I am not surprised about you two. I don't feel a thing. I am quite willing to stay here and watch you die with hunger. And you are not going to give me syphilis.

SHAKIE: LICK THEM SOBERS! My father die with syphilis in his blood.

STUMPIE: Look what the last Jew woman done to me before I was twenty-one. She kept me in Golders Green, a well-fed stud man for a year, and make me feel that there was nothing sweeter than sucking cock and pussy. She went on her knees begging me never to leave her. Then she would have me fucking her on her rug every Sunday, in front of a coal fire. Then, when I willingly fall in love with her, that was the day she start fucking another black man, and set off a whole series of concussion in my head. Two black men fucking the same white woman, that was too much for me. I threatened to kill her. She give me a one-way air ticket to Germany. I take it and walk from Germany to Africa, and found peace. There is no reason why a black man should not sell a middle-class black woman to a retired white man, since all she live for is to fuck with them for nothing. We need money to do good black people business.

SHAKIE: Damn right Stumpie! Some nice rich white man is waiting in his shop down King's Road. We even have our eyes on a special one, and he's hoping we will take you to visit him so that he can take off with you on his winter cruise in the West Indies. Then, when he returns, we will make enough profit from his business to set up our own business in Africa. So go and get ready and let us get it over with!

JACKIE: I will kill myself first!

STUMPIE: It could be written in the law books never to trust a woman! So it is fitting and proper to sell them, even if they only have potential middle-class backgrounds. 'For ever, SING IT LOUD! I want to talk with you.' Those were the words of the soul singer.

JACKIE: You have to kill me before you get me out of this house. It's in your blood, murdering people for their money. I am not interested in black power politics – grabbing and taking with no moral or sympathy. I refuse to give you any of my money. So you are willing to start the slave trade all over again by selling me?

STUMPIE: This woman is no fool. She only need guidance which we are prepared to give her. Madam, you could change your mind and join us in helping us to catch a few of those slinky black girls walking King's Road day and night. Believe me, you are only stopping them from giving away their assholes to white Rolls Royce.

SHAKIE: Come on, Jackie, get your furs and pretty jewels! The man is waiting. It is no use stalling. Nothing is going to change until you accompany us to the King's Road.

STUMPIE: The only reason we don't drag you out of here by your hair is we don't want to bruise you. We cannot afford to damage a valuable property like you.

JACKIE: How much money do you need?

SHAKIE: (*Leaps to his feet.*) Millions! LICK THEM RASS CLATH SOBERS! John saw them coming! We are about to leave the land of Babylon. Thanks for reminding me that my father die of syphilis. It's women like you who spread VD all over the country while Barclays Bank manager smiles at your large bank account. You fucking take good poor people money from the West Indies to buy old clothes down the King's Road. I want enough money to turn up in Africa for the next mass funeral of the blacks. I want to see the white man ripping out their eyeballs and their cock away from their body, and bury them with only half of their body in the ground, and the vultures eating the other half away. For the sake of money to store away in Barclays Bank. Millions of blacks must be buried so that millions of pounds can be added to Barclays Bank profit. We were late for the fifteen thousand the British government killed in Kenya.

STUMPIE: I must congratulate the Americans on the hygienic way they use to dispose of the blacks. They push stakes through their assholes and penetrate their neck and brains, put them on spits, roast them until shit and corruptions spill from their guts, and the white children stand around and enjoy themselves watching the bonfire while they are eating their sandwiches. Next time when we kneel in our churches to pray to God, and the fucking soldiers, them shoot us down in the back, I want to be there when the roll is calling.

SHAKIE: Get your Barclaycard, Miss Jackie! You have got a lot of Barclays bankers to visit today. Never again will we put our eggs in one basket. If our client doesn't pay up, a couple of your Barclays Bank managers will have to help us out.

JACKIE: Take everything! Just let me get away from here. You know where my handbag is. Take everything you find in it. Which newspaper in the world would believe this story? The two of you will be praying for a death that will never come. Syphilis will not kill you. You will be rotten before you are dead!

STUMPIE: Shut up! Look how wicked you are, pretending to be black when you wish you was white as Father Christmas. You are right, the sins of the father shall follow the children. The syphilis that you keep talking about will finish where it started – right here in Babylon. All we want from you is to help a few of the starving black people who is running away from gun bullet all over the world. We want to hear a few of their last words. Come, Shakie, let's organise the day. Get the woman ready!

JACKIE: I am going nowhere! I will give you all the money I can lay my hands on if you will guarantee my safe return to Priscilla.

STUMPIE: Do you think we are the government? What guarantee can we give you?

SHAKIE: We could wish her good luck.

JACKIE: What is this I am subjected to? I can't even get a word in over my own money which my father give to me. Father, father, what a bitter ending!

SHAKIE: Somebody have to suffer. My hard-earned, good
English money, lost to a bunch of sixty-year-old middle
class beatniks who is going to use it to eat raw meat in
some Italian restaurant and drink Mr Rothschild's '49
red wine!

STUMPIE: Yes, sir! And not a penny of it will be allocated
to the poor blacks.

SHAKIE: Jackie, go and change your dirty underwear.
I am a fascist black man. I want to get to the motherland.
Yes, the African drum is calling. We must leave this very
day for Africa, and you are the only one can help us.
Stumpie, go and get the Bible. I want to read her a
certain chapter in Jeremiah.

STUMPIE: No man, we haven't got the time!

JACKIE: You have got all the time in the world. The fifteen
thousand that you want, I don't have that much money in
the bank, and no bank manager is going to lend me that
much money. What are you doing to me? I am not your
slave. I don't even know what day it is. I can't think
straight. Please go away and leave me alone. I've done
nothing wrong except buy your father a decent wreath
for his funeral. (*Beginning to get hysterical.*) I am not going
to scream for help. I am too weak and nervous to
scream. Your dead father will kill you for this! There is
no word in the dictionary to describe what you are doing
to me. I feel so dirty, I even lost my sense of smell. Oh
God! I feel dirty! I can't even go to the toilet; as soon as
I drop my drawers you will rape me! I can't go on much
longer! I will give you every penny I've got in the bank.
Please, any other life except this! What should I do?

STUMPIE: Talk to her, Shakie.

SHAKIE: No, man, let she finish what she want to say.

JACKIE: What will I tell Priscilla? Her delinquent father
rob her life savings? I must talk to a sane person. Please
open the door and let's go!

SHAKIE: So you are not going to change your dirty
underwear?

JACKIE: No!

STUMPIE: Shakie, you better talk to the woman. They will lock us up the minute we step outside, with her dressed like that!

SHAKIE: Go and change, Jackie.

JACKIE: No, God, no! You will only rape me! Anything but having sex with you! Please, Okay. I will go and change. But please, let's leave the minute I'm ready!

SHAKIE: Nice one Cyril! LICK THEM RASS CLATH SOBERS!

STUMPIE: Yes Lord! She's ready for the pickin'.

JACKIE: You are both young, but you must realise that you are going to be grown men in the near future. I personally can forgive you both for what you are doing to me. Well, what is life all about? Maybe I can live without my money, I don't know. And that's the way it is. There is nothing you two can do for black people that greater men than yourselves haven't tried before. Once, in London, when I was going to boarding school, a whole bunch of us girls was out sightseeing for the day. I had no idea what it was like to be a poor black girl. On the tube station I saw a young beautiful black girl sweeping the station. I could not stop myself from attacking her with the broom she was sweeping with. If black men is suffering, then what is happening to black women? I thought I was beautiful until I see that girl sweeping the station. Then I realised how ugly I was. No regrets. Do you mind if I go to the toilet before I change? If ever you see your daughter in the future, you are going to have a lot of explanation to do. (*She exits.*)

STUMPIE: There is no wrong or right left in this world. Just grab what you can get.

SHAKIE: Yeah.

(*JACKIE enters.*)

JACKIE: What have you done with my handbag?

SHAKIE: What handbag?

JACKIE: My bloody handbag.

SHAKIE: Why you getting so hysterical about your handbag?

STUMPIE: I know where it is. I was having a look at your perfume last night. Well you smell so nice I had to check it out.

JACKIE: Where is it?

STUMPIE: When we are ready to leave I will give it to you.

SHAKIE: Tell her where it is, man.

STUMPIE: Alright. It's next to the door on the floor in the bathroom.

JACKIE: I think both of you have made a terrible mistake.

SHAKIE: Don't start that shit again. It's over and done with. You can stay here and keep patronising the old King's Road and end up eating your own shit before you are fifty.

JACKIE: Yes of course. Thank you both for everything.

STUMPIE: That's very kind of you. Just try and be a little helpful sweetheart. We will not forget your good deeds.

JACKIE: Yeah. (*She laughs hysterically.*) You know, I really believe you two is wicked enough to sell me and get away with it. Well well. So this is the big break you gentlemen has been waiting for. At least let's drink another bottle of champagne to celebrate.

STUMPIE: (*Getting bottle of champagne.*) Madam, it will give me great pleasure to pour you a glass of champagne.

JACKIE: Tell me, Stumpie, don't you see that Shakie's working you to death while he's sitting on his fat ass doing nothing. Let him do some of the dirty work, like satisfying my passion, for a change.

STUMPIE: I can do that. I am more healthier than him.

SHAKIE: Well, you two can stay here and drink champagne. I will take a walk down the King's Road to check up on Jackie's old man with the money.

JACKIE: For God's sake, you're not going to leave me alone with this woman-beater? While you was out last night I had to lock the bedroom door because he was trying to get into bed with me.

SHAKIE: That is nothing to worry yourself about. Me and Stumpie screw one woman the same time not long ago.

JACKIE: I am not afraid, you know.

STUMPIE: I already know that. You are too wicked to be afraid of anything.

SHAKIE: Watch her, Stumpie, don't let her out of your
      sight. I'll be as quick as I can.

STUMPIE: Right brother. Take care on your journey. God
      go with you. And hurry back.

SHAKIE: Right. (*He exits.*)

JACKIE: If you lay one finger on me while he's out I will
      kill you. Please refill my glass.
      (*STUMPIE pours champagne into her glass.*)
      Now that you two genius is about to achieve your
      life-long ambition, I think the time has come for me to
      rest my heart in peace and enjoy the luxurious life that is
      ahead of me. Could you possibly make me a joint? I am
      sure it will stop me from getting hysterical.

STUMPIE: There is nothing to get hysterical about.
      (*He gets papers etc. to make the joint.*) I wish I was a woman.
      All women like you have to do is open your legs and
      men come running by the dozen. And anyway, in a few
      years time, when your old man dies, you'll be resaleable
      at a profit.

JACKIE: Have you any other suggestions? Well, for
      example, what should I do about my baby, Priscilla?
      Abandon her, I suppose? What about the joint? Haven't
      you finished it yet?

STUMPIE: Yes, coming up. As far as I see to rass clath,
      she's in Jamaica while you are in England giving away
      pussy from one end of King's Road to the other.

JACKIE: Come to think of it, what you two are doing is
      quite straightforward: murdering my body for money.

STUMPIE: No no, we are not murdering your body. We are
      only selling it without a bill of sale.

JACKIE: (*Screams.*) Oh, God! My belly button is burning
      me. I can't keep still. I am shaking. No no, it's not true,
      it's only a dream. Why did I come back to this place?

STUMPIE: Listen, if you have any complaint about what's
      going on, complain to Shakie and don't tell me about it.
      Every time I look at women like you I only see money.
      Money, money. I want money to do my business. I want
      rass clath money; money to get me to Africa – money to

put a smile on my face. I don't care when I die or how
I die as long as I got money. I am a soldier for money
and I'm willing to die on the battlefields for money.
Ever since the day I had enough money to buy my first
'Melody Maker', I wanted money to promote black
people's music. Black people's music must live! Money,
money to rass cloth to keep the wheels turning. The
continent of Africa need money to promote black
people's music.

JACKIE: Well, Stumpie, you finally convince me.
(*STUMPIE makes to hand her the joint.*)
Would you please light the joint for me?
(*STUMPIE lights the joint.*)
Is one thing I know, after the deal is gone through,
nothing else can happen to me.
(*STUMPIE hands her the joint. She inhales.*)
My God! So this is what the herb tastes like? It's light,
isn't it? What will it do to me? The joint, I mean.

STUMPIE: It will make you see the light.

JACKIE: 1974 is my year. I own 1974. Yes, you convince me
some more. The joint tastes quite nice. Maybe I should
have smoked my first joint a long time ago. Still, I am
not too late to make it to the other side of the river.
There is one little point that is bothering me; tell me
something, don't you have no respect for me, eh, as a
black woman?

STUMPIE: Would you like me to answer that?

JACKIE: No, no, you don't have to. Why is that boy taking
such a long time to come back? My God, a boy is the
father of my Priscilla. A fucking little boy is the father
of my baby Priscilla! Music! Music. That's it, play some
music, Stumpie.

STUMPIE: The record player is there. Help yourself.

JACKIE: Do you know, I am entitled to know how much
money you are selling me for.

STUMPIE: Don't worry yourself about that. We will get
enough.

JACKIE: Yes. That was a stupid question. Did you know
I haven't eaten for three days? But I am not complaining

144

because I am not hungry. I have always thought I could explain myself at any level. But how was I to know that two teenage delinquents was planning to sell me? God I am so stink! Anyone can smell me from miles around. Yet I got trunks and trunks filled with clean clothes. Doesn't my smelly body offend you?

STUMPIE: Do you think I am stupid? Money doesn't smell. It just bring joy and comfort to underprivileged black people like myself.

JACKIE: Oh yes, the joint is quite nice. But I must go and get changed for the sale of the century. My handbag. Where is it?

STUMPIE: In the bathroom.

JACKIE: Yes, I almost forget. Would you like to finish the joint?

STUMPIE: No, you keep it. It's nice to have a smoke in the bath.

JACKIE: Jamaica Jamaica! Right, I am off to the bathroom. I still wouldn't mind if you play a record for me.

STUMPIE: Alright. You go and get changed. I will play a record.

(*He puts on a tape*: '*The Harder They Come*' *by Jimmy Cliff*.)

JACKIE: That's a very nice tune. I hope you two get a decent price for my body.

STUMPIE: We will.

JACKIE: Yes, I know.

(*SHAKIE enters*.)

My baby father. I am just off to get changed.

SHAKIE: What's the matter with her?

STUMPIE: I don't know. But I just give her her first joint.

SHAKIE: What? You're not serious. What, Jackie smoking her first joint? You mean you have changed her life in the few minutes I have left?

STUMPIE: Yes, man, she draw the ganja joint as good as any rasta man.

SHAKIE: Rass clath, Stumpie! I've seen the box of money with my own eyes. The white man got a box of ten-pound note waiting for us. The man is just dying to get his hands on Jackie.

STUMPLE: (*Jumps in the air.*) Far out to rass cloth!

SHAKIE: He said that Jackie remind him of Shirley Bassey. Hurry up, Jackie. We are in a hurry.

JACKIE: Okay. I shan't be two ticks.

SHAKIE: Blood cloth. She's very cooperative all of a sudden.

STUMPIE: Yes, man. It's the ganja spliff. And I think she finally understand our problem. Ganja has finally help us to achieve our aims.

SHAKIE: Boy rass cloth. I don't know how I feel. Why the rass cloth are we doing all this for money? (*He collapses onto the floor.*) Sobers! Sobers! Garfield Sobers, the master cricketer help me.

STUMPIE: Man, stop talking shit. I haven't read many books, but the few that I have read teach me a lot. I know what you're thinking. You feel guilty because you are selling your baby mother. Guilty conscience never get you anywhere these days. Italy is one of the poorest country in Europe, yet the Mafia control America. The Jews, who doesn't have a land of their own except what the Bible give to them, and yet the Jews still managed to control most of white people's money. The Indian got it together, that's why General Amin expelled them. Yet the black man, with the continent of Africa at his disposal cannot get together enough paper money to promote their own black music. And just look at the amount of gold and diamonds that comes out of Africa every day. Fuck man! I don't feel sorry for one middle-class black woman. She's your baby mother, but she's a fucking whore. I am sure she realise that we are only selling her for the sake of black people. We are from the ghetto. We have no future unless we pack up and go home to Mother Africa.

SHAKIE: Darkness. Darkness. Fog in London. Garfield Sobers, shine some of your West Indian sunshine on us this day! When I was younger, I used to ask my father a lot of questions, but he was never able to answer most of them.

(*Sound of bath water running.*)

My father did everything the hard way, but I aim to do it

the easy way. But what is right from wrong? When the roll is called up yonder not many will be there to answer the right questions. Run, run for your life. Oh, Lord, give us this day our daily bread. Boy, she really look desperate.

STUMPIE: I don't know why she should look so desperate. Because she have a much better future than us. Old men will always take good care of her. But after this, if we don't make it to Africa, it will be the end of us.

SHAKIE: When you searched her handbag, what did you find in it?

STUMPIE: Nothing. Women things. Perfume, lipstick, nail file, you know, odd things – chequebooks, razorblades...

SHAKIE: Razorblades? (*He exits quickly, then rushes back.*) Jesus Christ! She's bleeding to death! Jesus, Stumpie! Oh, God, Stumpie! Ambulance! Quick! She cut her wrists! Oh, God, help me man!

STUMPIE: Oh, God, what?

SHAKIE: The ambulance! PHONE!

(*Blackout.*)

The End.

LONELY COWBOY

Characters

FLIGHT
5ft 11 ins – 6 ft tall, aged 28, dressed in
overalls, jeans, pullover, shoes

GINA
5ft 4 ins, aged 26, Afro hairstyle,
bangles, necklace, overall, flower dress, flat shoes

THELMA
5ft 5 ins – aged 24-26, Afro hairstyle, short furry
winter coat, jeans, blouse, earrings, bracelet, bangles,
necklace, watch, handbag, rings, high-heel shoes

CANDY
aged 18-19, Rasta hairstyle,
army fatigues, tall boots

WALLY
5ft 6 ins, aged 24-26, jeans, pullover,
lumber jacket, ring, watch, necklace, bracelet

DALTON
5ft 10 ins, aged 21-23, Rasta hairstyle, army
fatigues, training shoes, shoulder bag with papers

JACK
5ft 11 ins – 6ft, aged 25-27,
dressed in police constable uniform

STANLEY
aged 23-25, dressed in suit, tie,
briefcase, watch, shoes, bracelet etc.

Lonely Cowboy was first presented at the Tricycle Theatre, London, on 13 May 1985 with the following cast:

FLIGHT, Jim Findley

GINA, Angela Wynter

THELMA, Beverley Michaels

CANDY, Joy Richardson

WALLY, Chris Tummings

DALTON, Sylvester Williams

JACK, Calvin Simpson

STANLEY, Trevor Butler

Director, Nicholas Kent

Designer, Jan McClelland

ACT ONE

Scene 1

Lights up. Autumn 1984.

Brixton, London.

All characters are English second-generation blacks.

FLIGHT and GINA lifting bag of cement. Paint cans, stepladder, toolbox open on floor, mirror on wall five ft by 14 ins, four tables, four chairs for each table, fridge, micro-oven, cash register, shelf four ft high, glass cup, saucer, electric kettle.

All furniture is covered with plastic. FLIGHT takes sign brush and writes in last letter for 'Lonely Cowboy'.

GINA takes plastic cover off furniture. GINA exits to kitchen and comes back with apron and small hat, towel, face basin with water.

FLIGHT smiles, rubbing his hands, flicks switch on and light comes up on 'Lonely Cowboy', holster with two revolvers. GINA and FLIGHT take off overalls. GINA puts on small hat and apron. She looks at herself in mirror. GINA and FLIGHT wash hands in face basin.

FLIGHT: This is it we are now open for business all roads in the world lead to Brixton's 'Lonely Cowboy'. (*He turns sign from closed to open.*) God. I wonder when we are going to get the first customer, should I go around the back and do a war dance. (*He picks up face basin.*)

GINA: No man, stay here and pray for both of us, before the tide comes in.
(*She takes the basin off him, exits to kitchen and comes back whilst he is holding his hands in front of him, as if praying.*)

FLIGHT: Yes all good ships shall sail this way. We must show the rest of England that Brixton disciplines us with some heavy manners, from now on when we sleep our eyes shall become our ears. (*He relaxes.*) Gina my princess I feeling funny and nothing aint wrong with me.

GINA: Yes my stomach is unsettle as well.

FLIGHT: A lot of the old time pressure is going to come down on us, now that we have open our base to Brixton.

GINA: We are going to need some kind of music to keep the pressure down.

FLIGHT: No man we will only harbour the wrong kind of youths.

GINA: Why are you making yourself so old, so what happen if a customer bring them own music.

FLIGHT: You understand no music or back to Africa politics. Never inside the 'Lonely Cowboy' and hear me again as I tell you before no body popping contest.

GINA: Look people are only young once. I am not going to be happy staying here with no music.

FLIGHT: Princess you is a 26-year-old woman, I is a 28-year-old man.

GINA: So why are you behaving like 42.

FLIGHT: Because it is the right way to behave. We will just have to make our own music in bed. Wait you're pregnant? A stop at no red light recently.

GINA: Look at me when you are talking to me. (*She puts one hand on her hips.*)

FLIGHT: A looking.

GINA: You think you man enough to give me a baby.

FLIGHT: So tell me something, why you hotting up the place?

GINA: Because you've not landed at my base line for a month to rass.

FLIGHT: Stop the sex talk and think about what kind of vibes you going to give off when you walking away from the customers. A selling everything in the caf except you.

GINA: Just clear off from me and don't start watching me. (*She walks away.*)

FLIGHT: You is a joker.

(*FLIGHT gets revolvers from holster, starts playing with them. GINA opens fridge, pours herself a glass of milk, humming a little tune to herself. THELMA enters.*)

THELMA: Woo waa we, it open at last.

GINA: Wha happened Thelma?

THELMA: So is when you open.

GINA: You's the first customer.

THELMA: Well sell me something.

GINA: What you want?

THELMA: Anything, just sell me something.

FLIGHT: You hungry. The soup not quite ready. (*He puts revolvers back in holsters.*)

THELMA: I want a drink.

GINA: You can have one of Flight's root drinks. So is where you coming from so early in the morning?

THELMA: Yes give me a pint of the punch. I coming from every pub in Brixton. I trying to get a job as a barmaid.

FLIGHT: You always trying to be a barmaid, but that can't hold you.

THELMA: So is what can hold me?

FLIGHT: You's too sexy to be a barmaid Look how many men running after you and I don't see you running.

GINA: Flight shut your mouth.

THELMA: You giving me joke early in the morning. Anyway the place nice, nice, nice. Give me my drink man.

(*FLIGHT gets two half-pint glasses with milky liquid from fridge. Pours them into pint glass.*)

FLIGHT: Be careful my juice don't make you call. Your man better be good or you will mash up in back.

THELMA: Man I have no man, just a little sideline.

(*WALLY enters with bicycle, big boxes on front and back, loaded with socks, shirts, hats and caps, shoes and boots, shirts.*)

WALLY: You open and never a day early, nice, nice.

FLIGHT: Don't lean your bicycle on me table Wally.

WALLY: That's alright. I hear on the news in the market Jack join the police.

FLIGHT: That is old news.

WALLY: Did you get the job Thelma?

THELMA: I don't know yet.

(*CANDY enters with tape recorder and music magazine, loud poetry coming from tape recorder.*)

TAPE RECORDER: Bang, bang, hold corn, hold corn. Bullet, bullet, bullet. Bang, bang. Hold corn, hold corn. My mind is made up, my soul will find peace when Brixton free the slaves.

FLIGHT: (*Shouting.*) Turn it off. Wally your bicycle, the place just open.

(*CANDY switches tape off.*)

CANDY: You see Dalton?

GINA: No love.

WALLY: I want to see him.

CANDY: I must find him. (*She exits.*)

GINA: They are in love.

THELMA: Dalton tried it on me more than once.

GINA: Is what you telling me?

WALLY: So Jack get posted back to Brixton. Still I have no business with no policeman whether I know him or not and on top of it Jack never throw a brick in the riot. The place look nice man. I could have been a successful businessman myself if I did not get caught up in the riot. And now Jack is a policeman. One of our own blood.

THELMA: Stop worrying yourself about Jack.

WALLY: No I can't. In days gone by we used to sleep and eat in the same house. Our parents was friends when they were alive.

GINA: Buy something in the place. We just open, give us some luck.

WALLY: Give me a juice. You make the juice you promise you was going to make, Flight?

FLIGHT: Yes, man.

WALLY: Yes, yes, give it to me.

THELMA: I will serve him.

GINA: Sure.

FLIGHT: Wally keep hold of your bicycle the same way a man keep hold of his Alsatian dog in the street.

(*THELMA gets one juice from fridge, gives it to WALLY. WALLY empties glass in one swig.*)

GINA: That's one pound fifty.

(*WALLY pays.*)

WALLY: His rass join the police, so he could become the biggest man in Brixton. I glad it's not me alone hate him. I going to stand and watch them boy beat him. Rass. When he come to harass one of them. Boy oh boy, the inspector want to post him up to the West End, and make one of them big time criminal fire a real gun after him. All I have got on me, except the goods that I am selling is me money and me knife. Jack can never harass me.

FLIGHT: I said watch the bicycle on the table man.

WALLY: Alright, alright.

(*CANDY and DALTON enter holding hands. CANDY with music magazine.*)

WALLY: Boy you two is coming as I am going.

DALTON: One love.

CANDY: This is the start of the new liberated roots scene.

WALLY: So what happened Dalton?

DALTON: Nothing. Boy I just see something a while ago that I did not like. I am a youth but sometime I am ashamed of my own kind. This mugging business must stop.

WALLY: Boy, is so life go. Well I must hit the road. Rass clath Dalton. You don't hear that Jack join the police?

DALTON: Yes man, everybody knows.

CANDY: Give me two cups of tea, Gina.

(*WALLY and DALTON shaking hands in different positions. GINA switches on electric kettle, puts tea bag into cup, CANDY pays GINA 40 pence. CANDY sits at table reading music magazine. DALTON joins her.*)

FLIGHT: Wally come out of the place with the bicycle and don't let me an you have anything.

WALLY: Don't lose your cool, I going. You cook yet?

FLIGHT: You not going to eat in here with your bicycle.

WALLY: Right, I going. So Thelma we can't meet up tonight for a drink?

THELMA: Not tonight.

WALLY: Alright, some other time. (*He exits.*)

FLIGHT: I am very sad on the most important day of my life. I can't seem to find me foot. I feeling ever so funny.

GINA: If you feeling funny, go and lay down around the back.

THELMA: I could do with a little job until I start my barmaid.

FLIGHT: You mean in case we get busy?

THELMA: Yes.

FLIGHT: Talk to Gina about it.

GINA: Well since he's not well – I hope it's not too much trouble Thelma.

THELMA: Gina come on man, say yes.

GINA: Alright, how much?

THELMA: A fiver for a couple of hours at a time.

GINA: Okay. Flight go and lay down before you drop dead in the place.

FLIGHT: I going to take a walk on the front line.

GINA: What front line? For God's sake stay in the place, we only just opened.

FLIGHT: Yes, yes, but I overexcited. I must go for a walk.

GINA: Excited, what? Laziness is creeping back into your head. Don't think I'm going to do all the work while you piss off all over the place.

FLIGHT: I got my business to take care of.

GINA: What business? Shut your wicked mouth. Are you selling ganja and running woman on the front line?

FLIGHT: Thelma, you see how much my woman love me?

GINA: You are lying, nothing is wrong with you. You should apply to Equity for membership card and go on to the stage.

THELMA: Well you must remember you are not a cowboy anymore – is the caf is the lonely cowboy.

FLIGHT: So which side are you on Thelma?

THELMA: I am on the right side.

GINA: Before the man stay here, and knead the flour for the fried dumpling. Christ Thelma, him know I can't knead the flour, my wrist is too weak.

FLIGHT: I am only going for a few minutes to spread the good news about 'Lonely Cowboy'. Yes, I now got my own base.

(*GINA serves tea to CANDY and DALTON.*)

158

GINA: Don't bring no ganja come back here.

FLIGHT: Thanks for reminding me, now I am a businessman I stop all those foolishness.

(*FLIGHT dances quickly, feet moving fast, twist and turn. THELMA looks frisky as if she wants to join him.*)

THELMA: Why the place so dead? Put on some music.

GINA: We haven't got any. Flight say no music.

THELMA: You mad.

FLIGHT: Mind is not you that is mad.

THELMA: Alright, alright, what about the music?

FLIGHT: We will review the situation when I get back.

THELMA: What black people is sweetly bossy when they have a few pounds in their pocket. You going to show me what to do?

FLIGHT: Gina will show you, I am going, 'bye babes.

(*He exits quickly.*)

GINA: (*Shouting out to FLIGHT.*) Remember the fried dumpling them. So you want to start now Thelma?

THELMA: Yes, right now.

GINA: I don't know what to do myself, we will learn together. Check the soup in the kitchen while I write the price list.

(*THELMA exits to kitchen. GINA writes price list at table.*)

THELMA: (*Off.*) It ready, I turned the gas off.

GINA: Come back out here.

(*THELMA enters and sits next to GINA at table.*)

Right, this is the price list. Try and remember it in your head. We have to charge some of them different prices.

THELMA: Something like service charge?

GINA: Yes.

(*THELMA and GINA deep in thought studying price list. Police siren, car driving past. DALTON reading poem. CANDY stops reading magazine and listens to DALTON.*)

DALTON: I feel the pain
My hungry belly
Not wanting white sliced bread
So ease my pain with justice for all

For the blacker if he is
The pain will disappear.
I trying to dig a poem out of my belly, you like
it Candy?

CANDY: It's wonderful, I wish I could write like that.
Everytime I listen to your poems I want to sing. You
should try and get them published.

DALTON: No man. I just want to read my poems to the
youth of Brixton and put some knowledge and wisdom
in their heads. After the great success of the riots that
leave us ten times worse off and poorer, we need a
change which should give us a new lease in life.

CANDY: Brixton to you is like some earthly heaven.
You refuse to notice the heavy pressure that is going on
all day.

DALTON: We shall make progress in Brixton towards the
Kingdom of Ja. And when that happens no one shall
have more knowledge about Brixton than myself. The
freedom train shall arrive and I want to be a consultant
along the journey.

CANDY: We need to rent our own flat. Do you expect us to
live in our parents' homes forever? When do you expect
the train to arrive?

DALTON: I don't know, but the more poems I write, the
quicker it will come.

CANDY: Have it your own way.
(*DALTON continues writing poem.*)
Excuse me.
(*CANDY walks over to THELMA and GINA. Sits. GINA
takes price list and exits to kitchen.*)
Well I must say. I never believed they would even open
the caf after all the trouble they've been through since
they buy the place.

THELMA: It look nice.

CANDY: Yes, very modern. Maybe we could start a little
women group since the place is so nice.

THELMA: Well I am busy at the moment, I got a job.

CANDY: Nice – doing what?

THELMA: Barmaid.

CANDY: That's alright. I must talk to Gina, we should have a women group.

THELMA: No man, give it a rest for a while, they just opened.

CANDY: I really miss the old group that we was in. I have never seen or heard of any of those men since the police take some of them to the hospital.

THELMA: Yes we all did went into hiding for a few months. It was the men who started the fight. That sailor was a bad man. He's probably alright anywhere he is. He wasn't any good. He was a bad man. He had no conscience or mercy how he gets his money. I know him, I used to sleep with him.

CANDY: If the group did still keep going he and his friends would have had us all in jail by now.
    (*Police siren. Car driving past.*)

THELMA: What, them busy today.
    (*GINA enters.*)

CANDY: Let me personally congratulate you Gina. Your place feel nice man.

GINA: Thanks.
    (*GINA sits at table with THELMA and CANDY. JACK enters, dressed in police constable uniform.*)

JACK: Morning all.

GINA: What are we supposed to do – laugh?

CANDY: Jack, you now cross Jordan river?

THELMA: (*Laughing.*) Jack, your helmet is too big.
    (*DALTON gathering his papers together.*)

DALTON: No, no no it's not funny. Come on Candy, let's get out of here. Not another minute. Come on, let's go.

CANDY: Alright, alright, I am coming. (*Moving quickly. Picking up magazine and tape recorder.*) You must admit, it is funny.

DALTON: Shut up and come on.
    (*DALTON and CANDY exit.*)

JACK: That wasn't a nice reception from Dalton. I hope things will improve around here.

GINA: Are we allowed to talk to you?

THELMA: Not me.

JACK: No, just sell me a cup of tea.

THELMA: Tea what. Drink some punch and put some strength in your back.

GINA: You don't see, he's not a human being anymore.

JACK: I am a policeman, I'm not going to lose my temper.

GINA: I glad to see you know your place.

JACK: Is trying, the two of you trying to insult me?

GINA: What? No man, insult the God of Brixton. Thelma, Jack can have the punch on the house.

JACK: Is bribing? You bribing me now or what?

THELMA: Why should we do that?

GINA: What are we doing wrong?

JACK: I don't know, you tell me.

GINA: Look, you want the punch or not?

JACK: Yes, but I would like to pay for it.

GINA: It is not for sale to you.

JACK: In that case, thank you very much for your hospitality.

(*THELMA gives JACK milky punch from fridge.*)

THELMA: This is no flat-foot hustling. This is a legitimate caf.

(*JACK puts his helmet on the counter and starts sipping his drink.*)

GINA: And not to forget how many different pieces of paper we had to sign before we could open. The name of the caf. 'Lonely Cowboy'. So we don't want too many policemen for company.

JACK: I am a citizen, I have the same right as any person in Brixton.

GINA: You have plenty more right than most of us.

THELMA: What about those on the front line?

JACK: Some of them could turn into good citizens.

GINA: With a little help from the likes of you.

JACK: We are not as bad as you might think.

GINA: I don't have to think nothing. Every individual are a group of people, don't matter who they are, think they are best for Brixton once they live here. Christ himself is the only saviour for Brixton.

THELMA: And he's not coming back.

(*STANLEY enters, with carton box measuring 18 ins x 18 ins x 12 ins. STANLEY looking at JACK – frozen. Police siren. Car driving past. STANLEY trembling.*)

STANLEY: Morning, excuse me, sorry. I don't know what to say. I am only passing through. I going.

THELMA: No wait, you look like a real good customer.

STANLEY: What?

GINA: Man, grow up, is only Jack, born and bred Brixton black man.

STANLEY: No, well listen to me. I don't know what to say. I mean one love to the brothers and sisters, but a black policeman is no rejoicement.

JACK: What is this? Who are you?

STANLEY: A visitor.

JACK: Typical.

THELMA: Leave Jack alone, his bread is well buttered.

GINA: We only open today for the first time.

STANLEY: So what are you doing? Hosting the annual police ball?

JACK: (*Laughs.*) I wish it was.

(*STANLEY puts down briefcase and carton box.*)

STANLEY: You see me, I is a real black man. Me, Stanley. That's my name. Sell me a piece of salt-fish and two dumpling.

GINA: We have salt-fish, but no dumpling. But what a man wicked like Flight, take up him backside say him gone on front line on the first day we open. Before him stay here and make the dumpling them.

STANLEY: Well let me have some bread.

THELMA: Take a seat, I'll bring it to you.

GINA: So Jack, what kind of police work are you doing? You are too rude to be community policeman.

STANLEY: (*Sits at table.*) Boy them give community work a bad name in Brixton. Every policeman is a anti-community person, 24 hours a day. They control everything and them mash up every little hustling us black people invented.

JACK: Oh my oh my. He does rabbit a bit. What are you? An undercover politician?

STANLEY: Yes, and I was born in Brixton and I just
reached back.

GINA: What – our first black MP?

THELMA: With a Brixton credential.

GINA: Every time you talk in the House of Parliament all
the other MPs them would tremble. (*She gives STANLEY
two slices of bread with piece of salt-fish.*)

STANLEY: Thanks. Well yes, could I have something to
drink. Yes, give me a cup of tea.

GINA: The tea's not ready.

STANLEY: That's alright, I can wait a few minutes.

GINA: It's not going to be ready for hours.

STANLEY: Since when tea take hours to make?

GINA: Since I say so.

THELMA: Have a punch, I mean roots drink.

STANLEY: Oh yeah. Give it to me.

THELMA: Right, it's very nice.

STANLEY: You are the roots.

THELMA: Both of us.

STANLEY: That's nice, I like that.
(*THELMA sits at STANLEY's table. GINA gets punch from
fridge.*)

GINA: So Jack, you're under attack.

JACK: No, not at all. I going.

STANLEY: That's the best thing you could do.

THELMA: Don't worry yourself about the police man.

JACK: Lucky man. (*Putting on his helmet.*)

STANLEY: You jealous?

JACK: No. (*Laughs.*) Morning all.

THELMA: You stand there and think you is going to joke
me into jail.

JACK: It's not me you got to worry about.

STANLEY: Every policeman is the same, whether they are
black or white. You sell your birthright to the Englishman.

JACK: I am an Englishman. Boy oh boy you have got
chips, mountains and pressure on your shoulders.

STANLEY: Yes I know, while you is as free as a bird.

JACK: One…two…three…four…(*He walks away.*)
five…six…seven…eight…nine…ten. (*Exits.*)

THELMA: Ah der you are, he's gone, relax.

STANLEY: What's your name.

THELMA: Thelma – and that's Gina. I am just helping out for a while.

STANLEY: So Gina, how comes you harbour uniform policemen in here?

GINA: It is not my business who comes in here, as long as they behave themselves. That's two pounds fifty you owe me.

STANLEY: Sure. (*Gets twenty pound note from pocket – GINA collects.*)

GINA: Thank you. (*Gives STANLEY change.*)

THELMA: You're nice when you're calm.

GINA: Thelma, I'm going round the back, if you get busy call me.

THELMA: Sure.

(*GINA exits.*)

STANLEY: This could be my lucky day. I know about the caf. Where is Flight?

THELMA: He is on the front line.

STANLEY: What is he doing on the front line?

THELMA: I don't know.

STANLEY: Does he have many friends on the front line?

THELMA: I don't know very much about his business except what Gina tells me.

STANLEY: What does she tell you?

THELMA: Come on man, what is this?

STANLEY: Okay. Okay. I should not question a pretty woman.

THELMA: What's that supposed to mean?

STANLEY: It means you is very nice man.

THELMA: You're funny as well.

STANLEY: You make me feel nice man. You giving me a kind of homely welcome.

THELMA: That's a nice thing to say to a stranger that is close to you.

STANLEY: Oh what a way I am so slow. I now just notice how beautiful you are.

THELMA: I operate at a faster pace. I notice how handsome you was minutes ago.

STANLEY: You making me taste sweetness inside my stomach.

THELMA: The bubbly stuff?

STANLEY: Yes we can have plenty of that.

THELMA: You making me glow in the early part of the day.

STANLEY: I don't know the runnings in Brixton at the moment. Where can we get a drink and a smoke? I don't want to go on the front line.

THELMA: Later. I want to hear some more about the bubbly drink.

STANLEY: Your glowing have overpowered me. (*He holds her hand. They stand and kiss.*)

THELMA: Do you like me?

STANLEY: Like you? You's the best thing I ever seen.

THELMA: Don't be stupid.

STANLEY: Stupid? I'm willing to put my money where my mouth is.

THELMA: Oh yeah?

STANLEY: Let's go up the West End and do some shopping.

THELMA: You don't even know me.

THELMA: What can I say?

STANLEY: Nothing, let's go.

THELMA: Let me talk to Gina.

(*They kiss. THELMA exits. STANLEY lights big cigar. Lights down.*)

Scene 2

Lights up. Three days later.

FLIGHT sits alone at table with ingredients to make punch. Lots of unlabelled bottles – Nestlé condensed milk, plastic bucket and half-pint glasses. GINA in kitchen.

FLIGHT: Gina keep your eye on the soup, don't let it burn, you know how easy it is to burn peas soup.

GINA: You don't see is only one dumpling in the glass case. Come and knead the flour, I can't knead the flour.

FLIGHT: Later, I haven't stopped working since I get back.

GINA: Next time you disappear you must make sure you
  play a game with the traffic.
FLIGHT: Oh Lord have mercy. Pressure, pressure.
  (*Singing.*)
  One bright morning
  When this life is over
  I shall fly away home
  Me say fly away home to Master Jesus
  Fly away home. (*Repeat.*)
  (*STANLEY enters with suit, tie, overcoat, carton box, briefcase.*)
STANLEY: You happy man?
FLIGHT: No, not really.
STANLEY: Well you sound happy to me.
FLIGHT: No man, business is very bad. Is rock, me rocking
  me head to get some money to go and insure me car.
STANLEY: (*Puts briefcase and carton box on table – sits at table
  with FLIGHT.*) Well, I will come straight to the point.
  We both need each other.
FLIGHT: What man, no kidding? Gina, come serve the
  gentleman. I got problems.
GINA: (*From kitchen.*) What's happening, somebody trying
  to rape you?
FLIGHT: Stop your chatting and come serve the man.
GINA: I busy.
FLIGHT: You're not as busy as me.
GINA: I work my backside off yesterday, and last night
  while you was farting about.
STANLEY: No hurry, I can wait till you finish man.
FLIGHT: Boy, these women.
  (*Enter GINA.*)
  Is why you so miserable?
GINA: (*Kissing her teeth.*) I tired. Oh, it's you.
STANLEY: Yes, hello again.
GINA: There is nothing in the caf to sell you at the moment
  – go away and come back.
STANLEY: What?
GINA: Yes, leave, I want to talk to Flight.
FLIGHT: The man come to talk business with me – what's
  your name?

GINA: Him name Stanley, he's not going to talk to you
     until I do.

FLIGHT: No kidding?

GINA: No kidding.

FLIGHT: Alright man, I see you later.

STANLEY: Okay. Okay. I see you spar.

GINA: Flight is not your spar, you is just another freak
     who comes back to Brixton to cause trouble and mash
     up the caf.

STANLEY: I'm not going to mash up your caf, and I am
     not a freak.

GINA: I don't care what you are.

FLIGHT: Alright Stanley, I'll see you later.

STANLEY: Okay Okay have it your own way. I will
     be back. (*He exits.*)

     (*GINA sits at table with FLIGHT.*)

FLIGHT: And what was that about?

GINA: One thing at a time. I feel like killing you.

FLIGHT: Why, what have I done now?

GINA: For what you done to me since we opened the caf.
     How could you be so wicked? The very day we open the
     caf you disappear instantly and never come back for
     days until late last night.

FLIGHT: Princess, I was trying to collect my money that
     I lend the man. The car need insurance. We only just
     open, we need a good cash flow.

GINA: If you didn't lend it in the first place, you wouldn't
     have to go back to collect it.

FLIGHT: You know I make a little profit on the money I lend
     the boys.

GINA: I don't know nothing. All I know is that you lend
     money to ganja sellers and you're not selling ganja.

FLIGHT: Oh God man, don't cold me up so early in
     the morning.

GINA: No ganja money did not help us to open 'Lonely
     Cowboy'.

FLIGHT: I don't know, sometime is only ganja money that
     is going around in Brixton.

(*Police siren. Car driving past.*)

GINA: When are you going to take life serious?

FLIGHT: You don't believe I'm serious.

GINA: No stay here and help me run the caf and stop driving up and down the place like a madman.

FLIGHT: I will stop when I finish collecting me money.

GINA: You know when you didn't come back the first night when we open, I think you was dead. I call the police station and I expect Jack to answer the phone but he didn't.

FLIGHT: Oh God, cool it man.

GINA: And no more regular Soho night out, we can't afford it.

FLIGHT: Alright, alright, what about Stanley?

GINA: And another thing again, Thelma did not spend half an hour in the caf after you left.

FLIGHT: Pressure, pressure, what about Stanley?

GINA: I coming to that, he's no good. I don't like him. He looks like a killer.

FLIGHT: Leave people business alone. I warning you. Leave Brixton people business alone and don't let me lose my temper. What else you have against him?

GINA: Let me start at the beginning.

FLIGHT: Out with it man.

GINA: Don't shout at me.

FLIGHT: Alright, alright, don't torture me.

GINA: Jesus Christ, what a big stupid bastard you is.

FLIGHT: Stop hitting my balls and tell me about Stanley.

GINA: Well as soon as you left, him walk in and give Jack one piece of cussing.

FLIGHT: (*Stands up.*) I going for a drive.

GINA: No, no, sit down. Sit down.

FLIGHT: I almost got a headache. (*He sits.*)

GINA: Him just sweeped Thelma off her feet, take her up the West End, buy her three spanking new dresses, one helluva overcoat and shoes, a right here so, me sit down, nine o'clock the other night when they come back with carton box upon carton box and show me everything. What is he? Shakespeare – Romeo and Juliet?

FLIGHT: I see. (*He begins stirring punch with wooden spoon energetically.*) He's that kind of man. So where is Thelma?

GINA: Me don't know, they left together last night.

FLIGHT: Wally get burned again.

GINA: He didn't stand a chance in the first place. Wally's not a fool – he knows her.

FLIGHT: So Stanley's a millionaire.

GINA: Don't get mixed up with him, that's all.

FLIGHT: Poor me, how can I get mixed up with him? I don't know him.

GINA: As soon as Thelma take one of the carton boxes back to the car he was giving me the eye.

FLIGHT: That's interesting. Maybe he wants to give you the same things that he gives Thelma.

GINA: Make him clear off from me.

FLIGHT: Anyway, my cowboy days are over – I don't want no trouble. So Stanley think him can kidnap my woman.

GINA: Make him think what him want – I don't care nothing 'bout him.

FLIGHT: I wonder what him want to see me about.

GINA: Whatever it is it spell trouble.

(*JACK enters, short leather jacket, open-neck shirt, two gold necklaces, bracelet, watch, three rings on each hand.*)

GINA: Jack, is it your day off? Are you join the drug squad?

JACK: I am not answering no question and I am not asking any. I just want a cup of tea and a chat.

GINA: You and your tea.

FLIGHT: Jack, taste this and tell me if it wants anything.
(*FLIGHT uses cup to pour drink into glass. JACK tastes drink.*)

GINA: Boy oh boy. Policemen are really lucky.

JACK: Yes, it's not bad. Good – but it could do with a touch more rum.

FLIGHT: Why rum? And not nutmeg? The man choose the most expensive ingredient. Alright – I have a little left.
(*He pours rum into punch, stirs and gives JACK full glass.*)
How it taste?

JACK: Yes it is full of goodness. How much is it?

FLIGHT: No man, you catch me making it, next time you pay. Gina, you want a glass?

GINA: No sir, me no want no punch.

(*FLIGHT drinks punch.*)

JACK: Give me a dumpling and a piece of salt-fish.

GINA: Flight, go and make the blasted dumpling them.

FLIGHT: I haven't finish yet.

(*GINA serves him. JACK pays with one pound note. GINA gives JACK 30 pence change. Police siren. Car driving past.*)

GINA: So Jack you know where the police cars them a drive to now.

JACK: I am here, how must I know that?

FLIGHT: Good answer. (*He begins clearing table. Puts plastic bucket in fridge, unlabelled bottles under counter.*)

GINA: I hope you don't expect us to give you information.

FLIGHT: But Gina, what is the matter with you this morning? Did Jack ask you for any information?

GINA: Well he might.

FLIGHT: Tell me something, you don't have anything to do? You have any information to give to Jack?

GINA: No, but I was thinking about Stanley.

FLIGHT: But oh God in heaven, what am I listening to in my base?

JACK: What about Stanley?

GINA: Well he was arguing with you yesterday again when he came in here looking for Flight.

FLIGHT: I feeling pain to rass.

JACK: Well I am used to black people trying to get at me.

FLIGHT: I feel stupid listening to the both of you.

JACK: Where is Stanley?

GINA: He is with Thelma.

FLIGHT: How do you know that?

GINA: That's no secret, everybody see them together.

JACK: So what about Wally?

GINA: Wally can't keep up with him, he's a big shot. Buy her carton box upon carton box of clothes.

JACK: He only met her recently.

GINA: It was like grease lightning. They just zoom off up to the West End.

FLIGHT: Gina, leave Brixton people and police business alone before people start calling you police informer.

GINA: This is no informing. This is domestic talk.

FLIGHT: So suppose people come in the café bar and hear you talking to Jack.

GINA: That is not one God thing, because Jack is going to come in here every day.

JACK: I might.

FLIGHT: You see you, you want to kill me.

GINA: 'Lonely Cowboy' must have protection.

FLIGHT: Any protection that is going to get done around here, I will do it.

GINA: You are not going to be here. You will be gallivanting all over the place, collecting money that people borrow from you.

FLIGHT: So you're telling Jack everything?

JACK: Come on now, you're losing me.

FLIGHT: Jack, stop the police talk man.

JACK: So because I is a policeman you think I is not a black man.

FLIGHT: What does black have to do with it? Murder is murder and police work is murder to me.

JACK: What murder?

FLIGHT: Murder, plain and simple that. 'Lonely Cowboy' is no place for controversy.

JACK: But murder man, what you talking about? You making me body jump.

FLIGHT: Everyman is free, so the law say.

GINA: I feel like Job with the amount of patience that I have got.

FLIGHT: Shut up man. You see, a black policeman must have his differences with black people.

JACK: So our parents didn't have black policemen where they come from?

FLIGHT: Brixton is different. Everything is jail here, even murder.

JACK: But why murder?

GINA: Yes and some of them will murder you in here for a penny.

(*STANLEY enters with carton box.*)

FLIGHT: Oh my God! Pressure brings on a thousand

mountains to climb. I say how far are we away from new
year? I must make a resolution.

JACK: Well, time to move on.

GINA: That was quick.

(*Looking at STANLEY, GINA exits to the back. STANLEY
comes close to FLIGHT.*)

STANLEY: I want to talk to you.

FLIGHT: Yeah.

(*JACK and STANLEY catch each other's eye, very tense.
Police siren. Car driving past. JACK exits.*)

So here we are then. You want to talk.

STANLEY: Yes, everybody seems to be giving me the cold
shoulder around here.

FLIGHT: Nothing to do with me.

STANLEY: I know that. I was born in Brixton. Went to the
East End to grow up and travel the world. And now I come
back to Brixton to rest.

FLIGHT: You look well off man.

STANLEY: Why, because of the suit and the briefcase?

FLIGHT: You seem sure of yourself and you got money
as well.

STANLEY: Let's get down to business. I can supply Brixton
with a lot of ganja.

FLIGHT: Listen man, come out of my place and don't
make me angry.

STANLEY: Oh, so you're afraid of big money.

FLIGHT: What money?

STANLEY: Big money if you become my partner.

FLIGHT: I have got a partner, she's around the back.

STANLEY: Look man, you've got a nice place. This is
where we can make a good start of something big.

Brother, my ship have come in. It is your lucky day.

FLIGHT: How – and for what?

STANLEY: Let's work the front line with some good ganja.

FLIGHT: I don't know the front line.

STANLEY: Yes you do.

(*GINA enters.*)

GINA: I'm going to the market to get some vegetables.

FLIGHT: Yes, alright.

(*GINA exits.*)

STANLEY: Right, back to what we were saying. I'm willing to get rid of the briefcase and suit any minute now.

FLIGHT: I don't know what you're talking about.

STANLEY: Ganja man, ganja.

FLIGHT: What about it?

STANLEY: We could supply all the boys in Brixton with them stuff.

FLIGHT: How?

STANLEY: First, we will just run through the front line.

FLIGHT: You is a farmer? Are you talking about home-grown stuff?

STANLEY: No man, the real Mcoy.

FLIGHT: Listen Stanley, I don't know you and I don't know if you are mad or not.

STANLEY: Mad? But what the rass you talking about?

FLIGHT: How can any one man supply all of Brixton with ganja?

STANLEY: Boy is you mad.

FLIGHT: Is who you calling boy?

STANLEY: You – I is a big man, boy. My ship have come in.

FLIGHT: Don't call me boy.

STANLEY: Boy to me, right now, because I am big.

(*FLIGHT punches STANLEY with his fist. STANLEY punches FLIGHT with his fist. Punch for punch – fighting. STANLEY's carton box gets knocked over, ganja spills on the floor, table, chairs falling over, both of them groaning.*)

FLIGHT: Fighting me in my own place. I kill you blood clath.

STANLEY: Is who you think you punch? I broke up you blood clath.

(*WALLY enters.*)

WALLY: Flight, stop the fighting in your place. Come on man, violence is no good.

FLIGHT: I tell you not to call me a boy.

WALLY: Man stop the violence in the place.

(*They stop fighting each other. Holding each other's chest with one hand.*)

STANLEY: I is a big man, why can't I call you a boy?

FLIGHT: Stop it, I tell you.

(*FLIGHT pulls STANLEY closer to him. WALLY moves
quickly in between them.*)

STANLEY: Why take it so serious?

WALLY: Yes, done with it. (*He pulls STANLEY and
FLIGHT's hands from each other.*)

FLIGHT: Wally take the rass cloth bicycle off my table.
(*WALLY quickly holds on to bicycle.*)

STANLEY: Alright. I done.

FLIGHT: Don't do it again.

WALLY: Boy, black people is really serious.

FLIGHT: Boy. I hope is not me you talking to Wally.

STANLEY: Jesus Christ, look what the man done to me weed.
(*He shovels up ganja with his hands.*)

WALLY: Is herbs that? Lord, what a lot of ganja. (*He quickly
shovels with his hands into the carton box.*)

STANLEY: Move away from my things.

WALLY: Alright. (*He stands up, quickly holds on to bicycle.*)

FLIGHT: This blood cloth bicycle.
(*FLIGHT picks up knife, fork, generally tidying up.
WALLY looks at ganja. STANLEY puts carton box on table.*)

WALLY: (*Shaking hands with STANLEY.*) You're bleeding
man, go wash your face in the toilet.

STANLEY: I'm bleeding?

WALLY: Yes, man.

FLIGHT: Wally, take the bicycle out of the place.

WALLY: Alright. I hitting the road again.

STANLEY: Thanks. (*Exits to back.*)

WALLY: Brother Flight, this is your base, no violence. This
is where you take off and land. If you mash it up you
will have nowhere to land when you finish flying.

FLIGHT: I know. Go now with the rass cloth bicycle out of
the 'Lonely Cowboy'.

WALLY: I is also a cowboy. The only thing is, my horse is
a bicycle. Right, I going.
(*WALLY starts to leave, stops dead at door, turns about.
FLIGHT busy, doesn't see him, WALLY gently leans bicycle on*

table, tip-toes. Grabs carton box. FLIGHT looks at him.
WALLY at door. Looks at bicycle. Police siren. Car driving
past. WALLY runs away leaving bicycle. STANLEY comes
running in. He sees the back of WALLY with box.)

STANLEY: Where him gone?

FLIGHT: You don't see I am cleaning up.

STANLEY: Where him live?

FLIGHT: I cleaning the place up.

(*STANLEY exits very quickly and comes back.*)

STANLEY: Him gone, where him live?

FLIGHT: I don't know.

STANLEY: Alright. (*Looking at bicycle.*) Him bicycle will lead
me to him. All I have to do is ask the right questions.
(*STANLEY exits with bicycle and briefcase. FLIGHT stands*
still for a few seconds, puts his hand on his head.)

FLIGHT: I am sure they are trying to mad me. Where is
the respect from these people? (*He removes his hands from*
his head.) Look how the man want to mash up my pretty,
pretty café bar. The first man him pick on when him
come back to Brixton is me. Christ the prison troubles
have now begun. I bet I kill one of these monkey rass
cloth idiots. (*He removes the holsters and buckles the belt*
around his waist.) Yes I must prepare my head to fight
these people. (*He plays with revolvers for six to ten seconds.*)
Is going to be rass to play between me and them. (*He sits*
on table and put his hands on his head.) I shall not fall
under the pressure.

(*Lights down.*)

Scene 3

Lights up. Later that day.

CANDY and DALTON sit eating steak, rice and peas.

CANDY: I must get a job, or some good volunteer work to
keep me on the straight and narrow road to find my
roots. Maybe my roots are not in Brixton.

DALTON: You are with Mr Roots himself! And Brixton is
my number one.

CANDY: I wasn't talking about you. I like your poems and so does a lot of other people. Listen. What about asking Flight to let us have this place and we could charge people to listen to you reading your poems.

DALTON: That sounds good, but this place is too small.

CANDY: Oh, I forget about your friends.

DALTON: What about the club?

CANDY: Yes. We will do it, on Tuesday night.

DALTON: It will be a great night.

CANDY: And we will be giving the youth them some good culture at the same time.

DALTON: You think he will let us have the place?

CANDY: Yes man, it's empty on a Tuesday night.

DALTON: We will go and see him when we leave here.

CANDY: Good idea. He's a nice guy. He will let us have the club every Tuesday night if there is no trouble.

DALTON: Yes, and with you working with me he might let us do our thing. Dalton rise again. My youth them always behave themselves.

CANDY: As soon as there is a fight, I don't want to know no more.

DALTON: Keep away from the violence before we get started. This is the good book telling us what to do.

CANDY: Well tell your friends them to behave themselves.

DALTON: Yes I will. I am going to do a great reading.

CANDY: Oh I would love to hear you read your poetry in the club.

DALTON: Right, we will do it.

CANDY: I think my mum wants to get married again.

DALTON: So she wants you to leave home.

CANDY: Well sort of, but she's worried about me.

DALTON: She doesn't like me, does she.

CANDY: Well you never have any money.

DALTON: I am doing Ja work. Where I man must get money from?

CANDY: Well even in church they have collection boxes.

(*FLIGHT enters, collecting empty cups, saucers and plates from table. He puts them on counter.*)

DALTON: Brother Flight, the steak tastes good man.

FLIGHT: Yes, it was well seasoned.

CANDY: The smell is fantastic.

DALTON: Let we have two root juice.

(FLIGHT gets drinks from fridge.)

FLIGHT: Is what win the two-thirty?

DALTON: Running Wind.

FLIGHT: Jesus Christ. I knew the horse would win.

DALTON: Yes I lose in the same race myself.

FLIGHT: Why don't I follow my mind, the bookies sting me again.

DALTON: Don't make them mad you.

(FLIGHT puts drinks on table and takes empties away.)

FLIGHT: No sir, I don't have much to do with them these days.

CANDY: Wise man. The bookie is the only winner.

DALTON: I only have one bet today.

CANDY: Bookie and ganja, mash up the older black people in Brixton.

FLIGHT: Is joke you making? The church have a lot of them as customer.

DALTON: Boy, I have nothing against the church as long as black people can find peace in them. So Flight I hear you discipline a stranger.

FLIGHT: The man cheeky calling me boy.

(GINA enters from outside.)

GINA: So Flight, you have a fight in the caf with that Stanley and tell me nothing about it.

FLIGHT: That was no fight, nobody didn't get hurt.

(GINA takes empties to kitchen. He gets 'Sporting Life' and sits at table.)

DALTON: How much is that Brother Flight?

(GINA enters.)

FLIGHT: Let me see – eight pounds – pay Gina man.

(DALTON pays GINA.)

CANDY: You ready?

DALTON: Yes.

(They exit. GINA sits at table with FLIGHT.)

GINA: What happen? I told you he was a bad one.

FLIGHT: He's not all that bad.

GINA: What is he – a ganja man?

FLIGHT: I don't know.

GINA: Come on, tell me what happened

FLIGHT: He called me a boy.

GINA: Well that's not too bad, you are a little boy most of the time

FLIGHT: Oh yeah!

GINA: What did he want to see you about?

FLIGHT: He wants us to make some big money together.

GINA: Doing what? Not selling ganja I hope.

FLIGHT: What have you got against ganja?

GINA: I can't stand the smell – is he a ganja man?

FLIGHT: No.

(*Enter JACK, dressed in police constable uniform.*)

JACK: Hello, hello. This is official.

FLIGHT: One policeman cannot carry out a raid.

JACK: This is no raid, just a few questions.

GINA: You alright Jack?

JACK: Yes, yes.

GINA: You want something to drink?

JACK: No, I just want to ask a few questions about Wally's bicycle.

GINA: Wally bicycle? What bicycle?

JACK: Well Flight might know something about it.

FLIGHT: What about Wally bicycle?

JACK: We got Stanley at the station.

FLIGHT: Yeah – what for?

JACK: Wally claims Stanley steal his bicycle from here.

GINA: What, Stanley's got a car.

JACK: Well he was joyriding around the front line with the bicycle.

FLIGHT: I don't know. He and Wally leave here together, but again I am not sure. I was cleaning up.

GINA: Stanley's no good, but I don't believe he would thief Wally bicycle.

JACK: Wally claims he's afraid of Stanley.

FLIGHT: Wally is a coward, he's afraid of everybody.

GINA: I wonder if Thelma have anything to do with it.

JACK: Could be.

(*THELMA enters.*)

THELMA: Jack you have a lot of guts to come here so often in uniform.

JACK: No, not really.

THELMA: Gina I am worried I want to talk to you.

JACK: Oh yes? What are you worried about?

THELMA: This is no police work. I am worried about the man in my life.

JACK: You mean men don't you?

THELMA: No, I mean a man.

JACK: You know that Wally want to lock up Stanley for stealing his bicycle.

THELMA: I never hear so much rubbish – what does a big man like Stanley want with Wally bicycle?

JACK: Revenge I suppose. Are you sleeping with both of them at the same time?

THELMA: You've got a dirty mind for a policeman.

JACK: No, not really, I just trying to sort things out.

THELMA: Where is Stanley?

JACK: At the station with Wally.

THELMA: What?

JACK: Flight have you got anything to tell me about this?

FLIGHT: Jesus, no sir, nothing at all.

JACK: Something fishy is going on.

GINA: Yes, I think so.

FLIGHT: Shut up.

GINA: Stop barking at me like some dog.

FLIGHT: Is who you calling dog?

JACK: (*Commandingly.*) She did not call you a dog!

THELMA: What about Stanley and Wally?

JACK: Would you like to come with me to the station?

THELMA: No thank you.

JACK: Oh well, I must get back. (*He walks away.*)

GINA: Good luck Jack.

JACK: Thanks. (*He exits.*)

FLIGHT: You like policemen?

GINA: I like Jack.

THELMA: Why Wally so wicked? Why he wants to lock up Stanley?

GINA: Jealousy I suppose.

FLIGHT: I am going to sell the caf. Oh my God the pressure is too much for me.

GINA: Quiet your backside. I own half of it.

FLIGHT: Would you like to buy me out?

GINA: I might.

THELMA: I want to talk to you. Christ, I am so worried about Stanley. He is too much for me.

FLIGHT: Since when you own half of my caf?

GINA: Since the government change the law.

THELMA: What are you two carrying on about?

FLIGHT: Gina, who owns the caf?

GINA: You do, but I want half of it.

(*THELMA lights a cigarette.*)

FLIGHT: It is my caf, and I will do what I want to do with it.

GINA: Okay. Okay don't take everything so serious.

THELMA: Can I get a word in.

GINA: Sure.

THELMA: What should I do about Stanley?

FLIGHT: He's probably a nice guy.

GINA: If he is, what is he doing in the police.

THELMA: That's nothing. He's playing a game with Wally. He can buy himself out of anything.

GINA: How rich is he?

THELMA: Oh, I don't know. He said I am the first woman he had a relationship with for over a year.

GINA: Where was he, prison?

THELMA: No, he was working abroad. Something like travelling representative.

GINA: So what are you worried about? He's a nice guy.

FLIGHT: I will be back in a minute. I'm going to the betting shop. (*He exits.*)

GINA: So tell me about Stanley. He never look like no representative to me – but he dress nicely.

THELMA: That's one of the things I am worried about. And he's too aggressive for that kind of work.

GINA: The way he was going on, I thought he wanted to put you in a bed of roses.

THELMA: No, he is serious with life.

GINA: A working man eh. They are very rare these days.

THELMA: Yes, but I feel something is wrong.

GINA: Maybe he's only kinky that's all.

THELMA: No man, what was he doing with Wally bicycle?

GINA: Yes. That's weird and he fight Flight.

THELMA: Is what you telling me? I didn't know he had a fight with Flight. Is one of my little friend call me just now and tell me that Stanley is riding Wally bicycle up and down like a madman.

GINA: Did you tell Stanley about Wally?

THELMA: What is there to tell him. I have never slept with Wally.

GINA: What? And I thought it was him who was blowing breath in your face at night.

THELMA: When I want to go on the front line I always go with Wally that's all.

GINA: Oh I see.

THELMA: Listen man, help me. I don't understand what's going on. Stanley park his car and ride Wally bicycle all over Brixton until he get arrested.

GINA: What Stanley tell you?

THELMA: Nothing. I haven't seen him.

GINA: Flight got the answer.

THELMA: Him like Flight. He said they would make great partners.

GINA: But how does Wally bicycle get in the act? Did he ever tell you anything about Wally bicycle?

THELMA: No, not a thing.

GINA: He just come to Brixton, pick you up, fight Flight and now he is in jail for thiefing Wally bicycle. I don't believe he's a working man.

THELMA: Yes I'm having my doubts.

GINA: Anyway, let's have couple glasses of punch.

THELMA: Good. The punch will make you mash up Flight
    back in bed tonight.
GINA: You see how life is sweet Thelma.
THELMA: Just make sure he tell you all his secret that's all.
GINA: Yes I will.

(*They begin laughing. Lights down.*)

End of Act One.

ACT TWO

Scene 1

Lights up. Four days later.

Night. Café closed. Curtains drawn. Everything is clean and ready for the next day. FLIGHT enters from kitchen. He is very tired, hasn't slept for days. He is walking around the café. As he speaks, his hands are in and out of his pocket. Sometimes his hands move gently, sometimes vigorously.

FLIGHT: My entire world have changed since I opened the caf. Things that I think was impossible is now happening to me. Blood clath. Like tons of bricks they all coming down on me. Something can only be described as a miracle. What will happen to 'Lonely Cowboy' if I let these people tear me apart. It is all hustling and killing in Brixton. As soon as you try to do anything legal. Nothing can change me mind. I'm not carrying no news about nobody. All I want is to run a good, honest business in Brixton, but no, every ball head is running to me with their troubles as if I am Ja. Can all these things be true? Haven't I work hard enough to promote myself above police station and courthouse? But what the rass is this? What is plainclothes policemen doing in my caf as soon as my back turned to do a little mini-cab work and one trip to Birmingham? What will happen to 'Lonely Cowboy' if I let these people drag me into police station and courthouse to give evidence against one black man for another black man. None of it doesn't have anything to do with me. I am not a news carrier, so I've got nothing to tell anybody. So I have got to stop do everything and just sit down and watch me café bar. The place haven't been open for two weeks and already plainclothes policemen coming here and write down my name. Tulse Hill will have to fall down in Babylon Brixton before I let the pressure kill me. Blood clath, the end will have to justify the means. Yes let the stamping carry on all over the place and I myself is going to do a lot of stamping if anybody come in here to rugby tackle me again. Every living person must realise that it was a lot of hard work to open 'Lonely Cowboy'. People on earth I work hard for the little I've got. Why should I let those bastards take it away from me.

(*FLIGHT sits. Enter GINA from kitchen. THELMA behind. They are tired, they haven't slept for days. THELMA smoking cigarette nervously. THELMA sits at FLIGHT's table. GINA standing.*)

GINA: I am getting tired of your mouth. All you said was that you was going to the betting shop. What do you expect? You left the place for days again, lying bastard. You run away because you know the police was coming to ask you question about Stanley and Wally.

FLIGHT: Wake up to all the pressure that is going on.

GINA: Wake up? I haven't been to sleep again for days and it's your fault.

THELMA: All the lightning and thunder that is clapping doesn't have anything to do with me. I am involved with Stanley. He is in jail, and I want to help.

(*GINA sits at THELMA and FLIGHT's table.*)

GINA: For God's sake, I am your woman and Thelma is my friend. Tell us what happened. Look, if it is big trouble it is better to get it over with now than later.

THELMA: I thought it was a joke until he punched Wally in the police station and that is the only reason why they remanded him in custody.

(*Police siren. Car driving past.*)

GINA: Listen, I was the one who disliked Stanley in the first place, but this is more than anyone can bear.

THELMA: You see me, if I am going to die, I want to know why. Yes I want to do everything with my eye wide open.

FLIGHT: Look I am not Barabas or Judas. This is Flight who is always flying. The name Flight is a mark of respect for the things that I have done. I fly away from everybody's business. This is the only business I have got.

GINA: What about the betting shop? If I did not threaten to leave you, the betting shop would have continued to mash up everything and there would have never been any 'Lonely Cowboy' for you to brag about.

FLIGHT: Who's bragging?

GINA: Everything is you, you. No respect or love for me. I want to be I loved since I am slugging my guts out.

FLIGHT: Are you saying I don't love you? So who am I working for?

GINA: Yourself.

FLIGHT: I never dream you were so wicked.

GINA: Wicked? What the hell you talking about?

THELMA: Look honestly, Stanley is in jail and I don't know what is happening.

GINA: Tell Thelma if you don't want to tell me. I don't care about your secrets anymore.

FLIGHT: Alright Thelma, what do you want to know.

THELMA: You know what I want to know.

FLIGHT: For God's sake leave me alone. I going mad to rass. Why didn't I listen to what Stanley have to tell me. I going to wash me face before I start balling the place down. Boy I feeling sad again to rass. (*He exits to back.*)

GINA: Stop calling yourself boy, you know you don't like it. Well at least we're getting somewhere Thelma.

THELMA: Yes, I think so.

GINA: He's cooling down. I bet he tell us everything tonight.

THELMA: Yes it will be a great relief.
(*Knock at door.*)

GINA: Who is that?

THELMA: Is not Stanley, he's in jail.

GINA: Flight.

FLIGHT: Yes.

GINA: Somebody at the door.

FLIGHT: We close, why they bothering me.

GINA: I don't know. Come and find out.
(*Knock at door.*)

FLIGHT: Alright, alright I coming.

(*FLIGHT enters and opens door.*)

DALTON: Hello Brother Flight. I passing and I see the light was on and I want to talk to you.

FLIGHT: Yeah, alright, come in.

(*DALTON enters with posters and leaflets.*)

DALTON: Hello Thelma. I hear your new man is in jail.

THELMA: It is not a joke.

DALTON: It is – why else would he thief Wally bicycle and then punch him on top of it?

THELMA: You know anything about him?

DALTON: No, but I hear him have money. You know, you women should stick to us local boys. You should know by now that all strange cowboys that comes to Brixton always hot up the place and then go to jail.

THELMA: Stanley's not a cowboy.

DALTON: What is he then when he hijack Wally bicycle with all his goods? Him is a bad cowboy. Him just ride the bicycle up and down on the front line like him mad. I never know you was so beautiful. Him jealous. It seems like you let him taste a little bit of love. Fucking sweet him.

GINA: Call yourself a poet with such a filthy mouth.

DALTON: No filth is in that, just facts. Anyway is not my business. Brother Flight, I putting on a little show in the Salt and Water club on Tuesday night, so can I leave a few hand-out on your table.

FLIGHT: Yes, man.

GINA: So why ask him and not me?

DALTON: What you mean?

GINA: Why is it that it is always men that is the boss of everything? And then always cause troubles out of hell hole on top of it. Listen Dalton, nobody's boss of me in here.

DALTON: Peace sister, lot of love. Yes Brother Flight, this show is going to be great. (*He puts one leaflet on each table.*) I going to pack the place out. The brothers them must get some culture from us the local artists. I hope to see you there Thelma.

THELMA: I don't like poetry. I don't understand it.

DALTON: You don't understand me?

THELMA: No.

DALTON: It seems like I will have to start taking care of you.
(*Police siren. Car driving past.*)
Jack and his mates are busy again. It's not going to be just
poets Thelma, some heavy music is going to fill the air,
but still I feel you will like my poetry. Brother Flight, this
is a dread poem. This is how the evening will start:
(*Takes poem out of his papers.*)
See the school children
Running up the front line
They are black school children
Running free
The white policeman truncheon
Shall not touch their heads
For Ja words
Is home for them
Younger than the youths
They are Ja school children
No violence shall touch them in Babylon Brixton
This is Ja ruling over all
His children
For peace and love is the wisdom
Of black school children
See them running up the front line
The black school children them.
This is where I get down into socomento rudiments with
me poem them.

FLIGHT: Yes man I hear you.

DALTON: You like it?

FLIGHT: Yes.

GINA: It's getting late.

DALTON: Well I hope to see all of you at the Salt and
Water next Tuesday night. So you are alone Thelma?

THELMA: Is what's wrong with you Dalton? I going home.
Gina, see you tomorrow.

GINA: Yes. It seem like there is nothing more to be gain
here tonight.

DALTON: Can I walk you home?

THELMA: Please yourself.

DALTON: Thanks Brother Flight – I see you.

FLIGHT: Yes man, alright.

GINA: Thelma take care love.

THELMA: A feel cold and tired.

DALTON: Snuggle up in my arms.

(*DALTON and THELMA exit.*)

FLIGHT: Why you believe I don't love you?

GINA: You have too many secrets man.

FLIGHT: Gina, that Stanley is a bad man.

GINA: No he is a working man.

FLIGHT: Working man or not the carton box that you see
him come in here with, it was full of ganja.

GINA: I can't stand that word. Ganja troubles upon troubles
to rass. I don't want to know nothing more about it.

FLIGHT: I feel a little sorry for him, it's me who should
have get the box of ganja and not Wally.

GINA: Shut your face. That only spell troubles. I thought it
was jealousy over Thelma. Don't let him come back in
the place or there will be murder.

FLIGHT: I can't bar a black man unless he cause trouble.

GINA: What more troubles you want? He fight you.

FLIGHT: That was different man. Let us see this thing
out together.

GINA: I must tell Thelma my mind tomorrow.

FLIGHT: Listen man, I tired of quarrelling with you.

GINA: Me too, but promise me you will not get mixed up
with my ganja business.

FLIGHT: Tell you truth, I don't want to lose you Gina.

GINA: I know you love me sometimes.

FLIGHT: No man, all the time.

GINA: I wish I could prove that. Life is only going to be
hard for us if we don't make the right preparation. I don't
want to break down in tears. Let us try and save the little
money we making out of the caf.

FLIGHT: But if him have a lot of ganja we could make
some good money in a short time.

GINA: No. He will kill Wally when he catch up with him.

FLIGHT: I feel Wally's going to disappear for a while.

GINA: Disappear what? He don't know anywhere else except Brixton.

FLIGHT: No man, him have money now, he can move into new ground.

GINA: I don't trust him. Why he thief the man ganja and then lock him up for his bicycle? That's when he should have disappeared.

FLIGHT: Yes, he's either wicked or stupid.

GINA: Both. I wonder if Jack know what is going on.

FLIGHT: I don't know, but don't tell him anything.

GINA: Don't be stupid, I am only going to talk to Thelma.

FLIGHT: Don't. You might cause more troubles. Make she find out herself. I will just keep on pretending that I know nothing.

GINA: Alright, let's go to bed

FLIGHT: Princess, I do love you.

GINA: I believe you.

FLIGHT: What do you say we lock up the caf for a week and go to the seaside? No I can't do that, I forget. I got an airport job tomorrow.

GINA: I don't mind. We probably can go the day after tomorrow. Come on, let's go to bed. (*She holds his hand.*)

FLIGHT: Yeah.

(*FLIGHT flicks light switch. Lights down.*)

Scene 2

Lights up. Next day.

Late morning. Chairs on top of table. Café closed. FLIGHT sleeping at table. GINA and CANDY sitting at another table.

GINA: No, it's not going to be long before we open again. We are just cooling it for a while.

CANDY: You mean they hot you up so quick?

GINA: That's life.

CANDY: We women should do something together. Men only cause trouble between the sheets.

GINA: I will do anything as long as it doesn't have anything to do with politics.

CANDY: What politics? Just a friendship that will benefit all of us. Look, I sorry about the caf, but I had to come and see you.

GINA: Yes of course, I would have done the same thing myself.

CANDY: You know when he didn't come by me last night I just know something was wrong. So as daylight I went to his house. His brother tells me he didn't come home.

GINA: Maybe he spend the night in the gambling house.

CANDY: I'm not having him back – she can have him forever.

GINA: Don't be so irrational, she's not like that.

CANDY: Oh yes she is. I hate her. She really gets up my nose. You remember our women's group, she fucks that up. We are friends, but she always seems to be the first one to get into trouble and look at this stranger that she take up with, he didn't know her for more than a few minutes before he was in jail.

GINA: Don't mention anything like that to her. She visit him every day while he's on remand.

CANDY: So what is she doing with my Dalton? Kissing and holding hands, when she knows everybody would tell me.

GINA: Maybe you should blame Dalton and not her.

CANDY: Come on Gina, she fell for his sweet talk as soon as my back was turned.

GINA: No man, she's not that type.

CANDY: I don't know, she's that type enough to take Dalton off me.

GINA: I don't think she would want to do that.

CANDY: I haven't seen Dalton for days.

GINA: Do you think he is with her?

CANDY: I don't know. I will find out when they get here together.

GINA: Listen man, you must cool it and take it easy when she gets here.

CANDY: Alright. I will try.

GINA: How are you getting on with the show that you are putting on at the 'Salt and Water'?

CANDY: I am beginning to think that Brixton people is not interested in anything like that.

GINA: Well I must admit that those sort of things have passed me by.

CANDY: That is wrong, it shouldn't.

GINA: Child, let me tell you something. Right now there is things that is much harder than poetry.

CANDY: All I hope is that all tadpoles will turn into frogs. Thelma really hurts me.

GINA: Candy, look at our café bar, we just opened and yet we closed already.

CANDY: I can't see what Dalton see in Thelma.

GINA: What a man can sleep like Flight.

CANDY: Yes, he's well away isn't he.

GINA: There is some dread troubles going on at the moment. (*Whispers.*) That Wally and Stanley business is very serious.

CANDY: Yeah – what you mean? I thought that Stanley was only mad with jealousy.

GINA: No man, ganja involved.

CANDY: Another ganja man? They are two for a penny these days.

GINA: But I don't think Thelma knows anything about it.

CANDY: What about Dalton?

GINA: What about him?

CANDY: Does he know about it – he's involved with Thelma?

GINA: No man, don't believe those things, but Dalton and Wally are friends.

CANDY: Yes they are friends. I wonder, I wonder.

GINA: Remember not a word to Thelma when she gets here.

CANDY: I feel as if I want to bad.

GINA: No you didn't mean that.

CANDY: She and her bloody one-night stand.

GINA: Listen, I am not telling you nothing but I know Thelma. A don't feel she would do anything like that.

CANDY: You don't have to tell me nothing. As soon as I left Dalton house this morning people was telling me about last night.

GINA: Don't listen to them. Is only hearsay.

CANDY: This is a dread place. Everything always happen at the same time. Oh Dalton, why you hurt me so badly?

GINA: Maybe he haven't.

CANDY: But how could Thelma do it? All I am doing is trying to find my roots with the man that I love.

GINA: Cool yourself and watch the dice.

CANDY: Alright, I will just give her a piece of my mind.
(*JACK enters, dressed in police constable uniform.*)

JACK: What is this? No service? Chairs on the table. While Flight sleeps his lovely life away?

GINA: Boy oh boy, you is one for the gab. We hard up.

JACK: Look more like bankruptcy to me.

GINA: All roads in your head lead to the courthouse.

CANDY: So Jack, would you give evidence against black people in court?

JACK: What is a policeman job in court?

GINA: He gives evidence against everybody.

CANDY: I suppose Jack believes he's got a grand job.

JACK: I have got a job.

CANDY: A job to beat us youth into the ground.

JACK: It was only in recent years that I was a youth myself.
(*Police siren. Car driving past.*)

CANDY: Your bells are ringing.

JACK: Yes, back on the job. So when will you be doing business again Gina?

GINA: Soon.

JACK: Well, morning all.
(*JACK walks to the door. THELMA enters.*)

JACK: Hello Thelma.

THELMA: What kind of foolishness this about Stanley?

JACK: I don't know. I am not on the case anymore.
(*He exits.*)

THELMA: I am getting tired of men. (*She puts her handbag on counter and leans on counter.*) I don't know what they do anymore. Morning Gina. You know, I feel Stanley's lying to me, but I can't prove it because he was so nice to me, but I can't take the pressure. So what's this? Why the chairs them on the table.

GINA: Flight didn't cook anything today. Have you seen Wally?

THELMA: Wally? If I see him, I wouldn't have seen him.

CANDY: But you have seen Dalton.

THELMA: Who are you talking to about men, Candy.

CANDY: You been sleeping with him?

GINA: Candy.

THELMA: I just come from Brixton prison to see one man, don't tell me about another man.

CANDY: Where is Dalton? You haven't jailed him have you?

THELMA: You little teenager bitch.

CANDY: Bloody whore.

GINA: Mice, mice, aah, aah, aah aah...over there!
    (*FLIGHT wakes up.*)

THELMA: Aah aah aah aah!

CANDY: Aah aah aah!

GINA: No, no, aah, get away from me!
    (*GINA, THELMA, CANDY holding each other. FLIGHT moves quickly, gets revolvers from gunbelts.*)

FLIGHT: Where is he – where, where? (*He runs all over the café.*)

GINA: (*Laughing.*) You wake quick man.
    (*FLIGHT stops. THELMA, GINA, CANDY let go of each other.*)

THELMA: You frighten me. (*She leans on counter.*)

CANDY: She shocked me.

GINA: So what were you going to do with the toy gun, Flight?

FLIGHT: I don't know. I just wake up.
    (*CANDY, GINA, THELMA laughing with each other.*)

GINA: How can you sleep when the 'Lonely Cowboy' is closed?

FLIGHT: I see. (*He puts revolver back in holster.*) So you don't have anything to do Gina. Alright. I going to open the caf. I don't need no holiday.

GINA: Good.

(*FLIGHT begins to take chairs off table.*)

FLIGHT: Let the war begin. I don't care.

THELMA: So Candy, what were you talking about?

CANDY: Dalton.

THELMA: Child, listen to me. Dalton walked me home from here last night and I hold his arm because I was cold. I haven't seen him since.

CANDY: Did you sleep with him?

THELMA: No.

GINA: I told you there was nothing to worry about.

FLIGHT: All of you stop your rass noise in the caf. Gina, you not going to the shops?

GINA: Yes.

CANDY: I'm going to look for Dalton. (*She walks away.*)

GINA: Wait for me.

(*GINA exits to back. CANDY waits at door.*)

FLIGHT: I don't care who get rich. All I want is the little that belongs to Gina and myself.

THELMA: So is who you dropping your word for?

CANDY: Gina.

GINA: I coming.

(*THELMA lights a cigarette.*)

FLIGHT: Me throw me corn. I man don't call no fowl.

(*GINA enters, wearing a short winter coat. She puts her hand on THELMA's shoulder.*)

GINA: I see you later.

THELMA: Yes.

(*GINA and CANDY exit.*)

You not just dropping words for me, you calling me fowl as well.

FLIGHT: I can't take other people's pressure with them bag of money.

THELMA: Everybody change since I met Stanley.

FLIGHT: And a lot have happened and a lot more is going to happen.

THELMA: I just met him by accident, but I like him. He likes you Flight.

(*FLIGHT finishes putting chairs down on floor.*)

FLIGHT: What for?

THELMA: I don't know, but I would really like to know.

FLIGHT: I don't know Stanley, but we know each other a long time.

THELMA: All Stanley will tell me is that it was a mistake to take Wally bicycle.

FLIGHT: He probably likes you.

THELMA: I know he does. He was nice to me for the few days I know him. I am sure he will get bail.

(*Police siren. Car driving past.*)

FLIGHT: (*Sitting very relaxed.*) I know that nobody can take another person to heaven, no matter how much we love each other. After death you are on your own.

THELMA: Don't talk to me about death.

FLIGHT: Yes, but people die for all kind of reasons. Can you imagine when somebody die with love to find their love that was gone before and only to find out that they were two-timing each other. Yes, you only can get to heaven under your own steam.

THELMA: Are you going to give evidence for Stanley?

FLIGHT: No.

(*WALLY enters, smartly dressed, mac, suit, tie, shoes.*)

I was closed a while ago, but I open again, but I don't have nothing to sell.

WALLY: I come to see you man. Thelma, no hard feelings. I tell you the truth, I'm not happy about it but I've got to protect me life. I really can't afford for anybody to kill me.

THELMA: You know, when I was a little girl I used to wish that I was a boy, but I don't wish that no more. You men give each other a hard time. Why should a man like Stanley take your bicycle, ride it up and down on the front line, then punch you in the police station?

WALLY: I don't know. I just got to protect myself. We're all cowboys and when you watch cowboys they win and lose a million every minute. So if a cowboy lose something he should take his pressure and don't threaten to kill people.

196

Is right here me born. Right in the middle of Brixton and no stranger is going to come here and kill me.

THELMA: So what happened? Is scank you scank Stanley or what?

WALLY: No man. I just talking, but I was going away. Still I feel a shooter is much cheaper than going away.

FLIGHT: Wally's what the rass clath you want to talk to me about?

WALLY: Cool it man. Peace. I is full of peace.

THELMA: Alright, Wally. There is things going on that I don't know about, but I might just find out one day. I going home. Flight, tell Gina. I will see her after court tomorrow.

WALLY: I am not going to be there.

THELMA: Who cares.

FLIGHT: Alright. I will tell her.

(*THELMA exits.*)

I want a long rope to hang some people to rass clath. So is try you trying to kill me? From you rob the man ganja is the first time I see you. Wally, I really love me caf and I want to keep it for as long as I live. I don't see nothing else to do in this rass clath place that I was born and I don't expect to get rich quick. Have you prepare yourself to meet Stanley your maker? I just open my caf and you just walk in here and thief a ganja man box of ganja and then half run away and get nowhere and now you are back to wait for judgement between you and Stanley. So what you come to see me about?

WALLY: I come to give you some money.

FLIGHT: Every day that I get up I make a little profit from 'Lonely Cowboy' and I would like it to continue that way.

WALLY: Man, I have made a nice little profit. I can afford to give you some of it.

FLIGHT: I must go and start cooking in a minute.

WALLY: So what you saying? You refusing my offer?

FLIGHT: Man, I want plenty more than what you got to offer me. How do you know is not my ganja you thief.

WALLY: Man, I am a born and bred Brixton man. I know everything.

FLIGHT: So is how long Gina expect to stay at the shop?
Did you stop and think before you thief the man ganja?
That plainclothes policeman was coming here and take
my name to the police station.

WALLY: Perhaps they want to talk to me as well because
news travel very fast in Brixton.

FLIGHT: But I haven't thief anything.

WALLY: First come, first serve.

FLIGHT: But what the rass this I am hearing. You cause
plainclothes policeman to coming here to question me
about your business, and now you come back in here to
give me fuck re argument.

(*DALTON enters.*)

DALTON: Yes, yes, it's cold outside but I just passing
through. Nice, nice. So what happen Flight? The place
feel real dead. You want to hear me read a poem?

FLIGHT: No man. So Wally I going to catch you later.
Candy was looking for you.

DALTON: Thanks. So Wally, you walking up the road.
Come on man, let's go on the line.

WALLY: Later. I want to say something to Flight.

DALTON: I came in with the breeze, but I'm going out with
the wind.

(*DALTON and WALLY clap right hands together and heavy
handshake.*)

WALLY: One love.

DALTON: Always.

(*DALTON exits.*)

WALLY: I feel say you is stupid to rass.

FLIGHT: You thief a man ganja and then come out with
your pretty beautiful self to wait for the man who is
going to come out of jail any day now to kill you. Yes of
course I am stupid to refuse your money. You'd better
leave Brixton for ever.

WALLY: Never. I will juk him rass first.

(*GINA enters.*)

I'm not going nowhere.

FLIGHT: Gina is what kept you so long and your arms are
empty.

GINA: I forget the money.

FLIGHT: So is what the men going to eat when they come out of the betting shop.

WALLY: Alright, alright. I see you later Flight.

FLIGHT: Yeah.

(*WALLY exits.*)

GINA: So what have you done since I left? You not going to start cooking?

FLIGHT: Yes. Let me cool off for a minute.

VOICE: (*Off*) We are police officers, what's your name?

WALLY: (*Off*) Wally, you know my name is Wally.

(*Police siren. Car stops.*) So what is this?

VOICE: (*Off*) We would like to search you.

WALLY: (*Off*) No man.

VOICE: (*Off*) Would you like to come with us.

WALLY: (*Off*) Sure, I haven't done anything.

VOICE: (*Off*) Okay Let's go.

(*Car drives off.*)

FLIGHT: Did you hear that?

GINA: Yeah.

FLIGHT: I suppose they only want to question him.

GINA: Please don't get involved with ganja.

FLIGHT: No I won't and I stop lending my money.

GINA: Thank God for that.

(*GINA and FLIGHT hug each other. Lights down.*)

Scene 3

Lights up. Ten days later.

Midday. GINA sitting at table with glass half-filled with red wine, empty wine bottle. FLIGHT leaning on counter opening bottle of red wine. He fills his glass and GINA's glass. He sits at table with GINA. FLIGHT lights cigarette.

FLIGHT: The dumpling them. (*Exits quickly to kitchen. Comes back with bowl of fried dumplings, puts them in glass case, sits, continues smoking cigarette.*) So tell me something now spar, how comes you like Jack who's a policeman?

GINA: I don't see him as any policeman, I just see him as somebody I know for a long time. I can't help it, he was always nice to me.

FLIGHT: That was in the past.

GINA: There is no future without the past.

FLIGHT: The world is divided. Some people on one side, some on the other. When Jack joined the police him choose to be on the other side. The other side I mean is that when he joins the police he choose to lock up everybody including black people.

(*Police siren. Car driving past.*)

And going to jail is not good for anybody.

GINA: But some people want to go to jail.

FLIGHT: And some of them want to go to work.

GINA: So how are you going to know who wants to go to work and who wants to go to jail, if it wasn't for the police.

FLIGHT: Then we want more social workers.

GINA: Brixton Babylon have more social workers than fly have shit to smell.

FLIGHT: Are you saying every black man must join the police?

GINA: The name police is going to be alive when we are dead and gone.

FLIGHT: You see what I mean. Jack is on the other side.

GINA: Maybe you are right about the world is divided but if a so it go a so it go.

FLIGHT: Now you take our little 'Lonely Cowboy', if we are not careful the police will close the place and that is no good to us or anybody else.

GINA: And there's a lesson to be learned from that, yes every day we all get a little more freedom because I know the police can't close 'Lonely Cowboy'.

FLIGHT: What freedom? Only a few black men that is walking up and down on the front line that haven't been to jail and is people like Jack who arrest them.

GINA: So if Jack didn't join the police force you don't think that the police would be still taking them off to jail one by one every day.

FLIGHT: Well as long as you know he's on the other side, it's alright. (*He pours wine for GINA and himself.*)

So Stanley come up in court today?

GINA: He's going to get bail. Where is Wally?

FLIGHT: I don't know nothing about anybody.

GINA: More troubles, what are we going to do?

FLIGHT: What can we do.

GINA: So do you hate Jack?

FLIGHT: No but I don't like the police.

GINA: I don't see the problem in your head.

FLIGHT: It's no problem. I going to look at the soup. (*He exits to kitchen, then re-enters.*) It ready. It taste iree. So you pregnant?

GINA: What pregnant? (*She kisses her teeth.*)

FLIGHT: Well you look a little fat.

GINA: It's your cooking.

FLIGHT: Well stop eating. I want to know when you're pregnant.

GINA: I don't know why we open so early. Nobody ever comes here until the pubs and the betting shop close.

FLIGHT: Yes, but we get the odd working men and strangers that come in sometimes.

GINA: Yes, but sometimes them never come.

FLIGHT: Well we must make sure that they come.

GINA: Stanley coming out of jail today, remember.

FLIGHT: Talk of the devil. See him outside a pay the taxi man, but if they want to kill us we will kill every one of them.

GINA: Yes, but no violence.

FLIGHT: Here he comes.

(*Black cab driving off. STANLEY and THELMA enter.*)

THELMA: Hi.

GINA: Hello.

THELMA: I am just going to get a drink. (*She kisses STANLEY and exits.*)

STANLEY: Well here we are again. I come to see you the minute I get bail.

FLIGHT: Would you like a glass of wine?

201

STANLEY: Yes, man.

(*GINA gets glass and STANLEY sits at table with FLIGHT. GINA sits at the same table. STANLEY pours himself wine.*)

STANLEY: Well, well, freedom again. But how can I forget. I suppose all of Brixton is laughing at me with my box of ganja. A sorry about our little differences. I did just come back. I was suffering from jet lag.

FLIGHT: So where is your car?

STANLEY: It was a hired car. I was suffering from everything. I am not used to driving on the left-hand side of the road. I was in the sky all the time, and now I am really down to earth. I am living no more double life. I am going to tell Thelma everything.

FLIGHT: That's good man. When are you going back to court?

STANLEY: Next month. Well I was stupid enough to go and look for Wally to kill him. Anyway it did not work out that way.

GINA: So you're lucky you're not on a murder charge.

STANLEY: Wally think him is going to get away with my box of ganja because him think he's a bigger cowboy than me.

GINA: I don't like ganja.

STANLEY: I hardly ever smoke the stuff.

FLIGHT: Stanley, I am a peaceful man who is finished with cowboy life. When you come in here the other day I thought you was mad and come to kill me when you was talking about ganja like it was something you find on the street for nothing. Ganja is on the street, but you have to pay for it. But now I see that you are working on some big ideas.

STANLEY: Yes, my ship have come in and it takes a lot of men to drive a ship. The little box of ganja that I bring the other day was only a sample. I didn't know ganja was as getting so expensive until I went into Brixton prison. Wally tried to fuck my head.

GINA: You realise that all this is putting a lot of pressure on Flight and myself. We are settled into our little café bar. We don't want no big time trouble.

STANLEY: You people don't understand how much you have been taken for a ride. You're only doing a little business because you want to do bigger business. I only ever talk about money or love for somebody like Thelma.

VOICE: (*Off.*) Flight, you dirty bombo cloth. You lock up Wally.

(*Brick comes crashing against door. FLIGHT moves quickly. GINA screams.*)

GINA: Don't go out there.

VOICE: (*Off.*) I going to bury your rass cloth in there today.
(*Brick crashes against door. Police siren. Footsteps running away. Police car drives past.*)

FLIGHT: I wonder if Wally pay someone to come and mash up me café bar.

STANLEY: This place is dangerous. It look like you going to need some protection.

(*THELMA enters with three bottles of wine.*)

THELMA: So why is two brick outside the door?

FLIGHT: Is any police outside?

THELMA: No. Why?

FLIGHT: Somebody claim that me lock up Wally.

THELMA: I just see Wally going in the betting shop.

STANLEY: Which Wally are you talking about?

THELMA: The one that you punch.

STANLEY: Now that I am in Brixton I have no intention of leaving, so I must protect myself. Which betting shop you see him go into?

THELMA: Come on, this is your first day of freedom. Gina do you know what is going on around here, 'cos I don't.

GINA: Let us all have a drink and forget everything.

FLIGHT: I just don't want to start bad again, but if I have to I will. Everybody's gone mad. I have become an invalid since I open 'Lonely Cowboy'.

STANLEY: And that is wrong. You should be living in luxury because it is a good business.

FLIGHT: Alright Stanley, let us stop pretending.

GINA: I going to move the brick from the door.

THELMA: Listen, if you two want to talk privately, Gina and myself can find something else to do.

GINA: Well I suppose there is no harm in them talking. So Thelma you know, Stanley is a ganja man.

THELMA: I know now.

GINA: I don't mind saying it. I don't like ganja business. Whatever business you going to do, do it outside the 'Lonely Cowboy'. (*She goes to door.*)

(*THELMA gives wine to STANLEY. STANLEY opens wine. GINA comes back with two bricks.*)

I will keep these in the kitchen to remind me of today.

FLIGHT: Did you notice that the guy who was throwing the brick was wearing a balaclava?

GINA: I never noticed because I don't want to know who throw the brick. (*She exits.*)

STANLEY: Well whosoever throw the brick doesn't have long to live.

THELMA: Are you going to kill somebody?

STANLEY: No, not unless I have to.

THELMA: You are more serious than I thought. I don't want to make a fool of myself, but I want to know what's going on. What kind of business you want to do with Flight?

STANLEY: Ganja business.

THELMA: I thought you was a hardworking businessman.

STANLEY: There is no harder work than ganja work.

FLIGHT: I feel sick again. I wish I did have guts enough so mash up the café bar. I can't take the pressure. I just don't know what to do since I opened the caf.

(*GINA enters.*)

All my power been taken away from me.

GINA: Stanley bring the rest of the world troubles with him when he comes to Brixton.

STANLEY: And I am not leaving it again, except for a few hours at a time to make my pick-up.

GINA: Give me the keys. I going for a drive. I have enough to drink.

FLIGHT: No man, stay here. I want you to know everything. I feel like judgment is only around the corner.

GINA: Look Stanley, your business is too big for us.

FLIGHT: Stanley, what exactly do you want from 'Lonely Cowboy'?

STANLEY: Well the 'Lonely Cowboy' to me is you and I would like you to help me sell some ganja because you know the place more than me.

FLIGHT: No, you're too hot.

THELMA: Why does every man that ever sleeps with me always lie to me?

STANLEY: I have never lied to you. So I am hot because that Wally thief my box of ganja.

GINA: What are you going to do about it?

STANLEY: Anything that I can do.

FLIGHT: I wonder who threw the brick, I getting angry now. I feel like killing one of them blood cloth boy.

THELMA: I thought you came to take me away to paradise. Oh well, I might as well get pissed. I don't know what's going on. And I don't care.

FLIGHT: But what a rass cloth liberty all these people are taking with my bread and butter.

STANLEY: Listen old man, now that you know my business I expect all of you to keep your mouth shut. I am now just another customer. I am heading for the top.

FLIGHT: These people start stoning me in the middle of the day. I going to do something about it.

STANLEY: You help me and I will help you.

GINA: No we don't need your help. All we want is peace in the 'Lonely Cowboy'. We are only a young couple trying to pay VAT taxes like anybody else.

STANLEY: But you're going to need help. (*He looks at watch.*)

STANLEY: Rass. It so, it late. I have got to meet a man in a few minutes. Do you want me to introduce him to you Flight? He could give you some protection.

FLIGHT: No Stanley. Right now I'm only thinking dread thoughts.

STANLEY: Well I going down the road. It won't take me more than a few minutes. (*He kisses THELMA.*)
See you in a while. (*He exits.*)

THELMA: I wonder why the police pick up Wally. They probably know everything.

GINA: They always do.

FLIGHT: I have been through some strange things in Brixton, but this one is different.

THELMA: So I've got to finish with another man.

GINA: He's too much for you.

FLIGHT: Jesus Christ. We haven't had one customer today.

GINA: What do you expect if people is throwing bricks at the place.

THELMA: I will have to tell Stanley when he comes back.

GINA: Do you think he will hit you?

THELMA: If he does, I will split his fucking face. Any man hit me again I am going to kill them.

GINA: I don't blame you.

FLIGHT: I wonder if I should go and look for Wally.

GINA: What for? He have to turn up here sooner or later. You wait and see. Everything will soon be blown away.

THELMA: When is Mr Right going to turn up?

FLIGHT: You know that this brick business is very serious.

GINA: Yes I know. I wish those toy guns on the wall were real.

FLIGHT: What should we do? Lock up the café bar again?

GINA: No we can't do that every time something goes wrong.

THELMA: And I am not going to do anything except get pissed. Finishing with somebody that you like is very difficult.

GINA: Since when are you interested in ganja people?

THELMA: Gina, I have no idea what is happening, everything is foggy.

(*DALTON and CANDY enter, holding hands, laughing and happy.*)

CANDY: Hello everybody.

DALTON: Yes, hello everybody.

(*No response from GINA, THELMA or FLIGHT.*)

So what happened? We can't participate?

FLIGHT: Yes man, have a drink.

(*CANDY gets glasses, DALTON pours wine for CANDY and himself.*)

DALTON: Everytime I get happy I just want to read my poems to black people.

CANDY: Yes, read the one you write last night.

FLIGHT: No man, somebody throw a brick at the 'Lonely Cowboy'. You know who it is?

GINA: Somebody's trying to kill us to rass.

THELMA: No man, don't talk about that.

DALTON: Oh God. Let Ja spirit live. You not serious.

CANDY: I am very sorry to hear that. Come on, drink up, let's go.

DALTON: So it really happened?

FLIGHT: Yes man.

DALTON: Alright, I see you later.
(*CANDY and DALTON finish drink and exit.*)

THELMA: Well, is back to my barmaid work from tomorrow.

GINA: I must admit I have got a terrible, terrible feeling. I just feel depressed and down. Why should this mash up our entire life? This is not pressure – this is death.

THELMA: Again she goes on about she undertakers.
(*WALLY enters.*)
Jesus Christ. Wally, keep away from the place. Stanley only come out of jail today.

FLIGHT: So Wally, how come people come throwing brick at my place and says me lock you up?
(*WALLY leans on counter and lights cigarette.*)

WALLY: Man is Stanley.

THELMA: Stop your foolishness. He was sitting down here when it happened.

WALLY: I get it on the news yesterday in the market and I check it out since then.

THELMA: He's only gone down the road to come back.

WALLY: Make him come back. He can listen to everything I have to say.

FLIGHT: Well talk and talk fast to rass man.

WALLY: Him come to set up everybody against everybody because he is really hot hot. Is hijack him and his mates, hijack a ton weight of ganja on the motorway. Me here say him take a whole caseload of ganja with him on the continent, sell it and then tour the world after that.

A sure say him want to set up himself in the protection racket business. Because you understand that is London man them him rob so they will be still looking for him. Maybe that's why he was in such a hurry to go to Brixton jail.

(*THELMA walks over to WALLY. Leans on counter.*)

THELMA: Tell me something, do you really know what you are talking about?

WALLY: The little ganja that I take off him was nothing. I was stupid. I should have waited and get more.

(*THELMA lights cigarette.*)

FLIGHT: So why does he want to pay people to mash up my café bar?

WALLY: Because him want to get into protection racket.

FLIGHT: Anyway, him soon come back.

GINA: You know, I don't think I will ever shed another tear, I will just band my belly and wait.

WALLY: Thelma, that Stanley's too big for you.

THELMA: How do you know what I want? (*She walks to the window.*)

WALLY: Right, it's not my business, but I'm afraid of no strangers in Brixton.

GINA: So what did the police want with you?

WALLY: Well they say they were looking for drugs, but they did really want to take me to the police station to ask me about my bicycle and goods that they confiscated. I don't want to see no police station or courthouse for a long time. You can tell Stanley that from me Thelma.

THELMA: Tell him yourself. Here he comes.

FLIGHT: Now Wally, I don't want no trouble in the 'Lonely Cowboy'.

(*STANLEY enters, laughing. Sees WALLY – stops laughing.*)

STANLEY: Wally, how nice to see you. Oh me, oh my. Let me see.

(*STANLEY's hand reaches into WALLY's inside pocket, comes out with big wad of twenty-pound notes. WALLY is shocked.*)

Well let me see, the ganja that you thief from me was about six weights. I will take about two grand out of this and I will give you the change.

(*STANLEY counts the money. WALLY takes a knife from his pocket and stabs STANLEY in his left ribcage.*)

FLIGHT: Wally.

(*GINA and FLIGHT put their hands over their faces and scream. STANLEY holds his ribcage with the money. WALLY stabs at STANLEY and tries to snatch money. THELMA screams and hits WALLY with her handbag. STANLEY reaches in his waistband and brings out a revolver. He shoots WALLY in chest. WALLY drops knife. FLIGHT and GINA frozen. WALLY holds on to THELMA. STANLEY fires bullet, it hits THELMA. GINA tries to get to STANLEY. FLIGHT gets there before her. STANLEY looks up. Fires. Bullet hits FLIGHT in stomach. WALLY and THELMA dying together. STANLEY confused. Doesn't know why he shot FLIGHT.*)

Oh God. Take the 'Lonely Cowboy' up to heaven.

(*He tries to reach gunbelt. He collapses. STANLEY doubled up. GINA snatches revolver from STANLEY and takes two steps back wards. FLIGHT dies. STANLEY moves towards GINA. GINA fires three bullets into STANLEY – he dies. GINA is frozen to the spot. JACK enters. Police siren. JACK takes revolver from GINA. GINA remains frozen. JACK looks at bodies. Looks at GINA and starts crying. Police car stops. Blackout.*)

The End.

Tell The Truth

A Tribute to Alfie

by T-Bone Wilson

The number of nights I battle
with my friend for letting go
the struggle, and he would
disappear for months – unfound
to work upon some model.
Then out of the hazy grey he
would appear and into my eyes
he would pry – how goes
the movement? And I would say
the movement is you, and he
would say – a true! a portion
of my contibution is on its way
– a play.

Yes I know him, yes I do, well
Not as a woman would but
as a friend should – for
when happiness strikes, God
Almighty and all the angels
would come down, and your
eardrums would bleed the hardest
fun from the hallelujah! hallelujah!
say it brother move it sound.

And the sweat from Clarendon
would exude and the tears from
Shakespeare's country would intrude
with wails, hails, like a monstrous
whale, and memories pass into
future would start the torture,
pressure, pressure, seems forever.
And God becomes lip-bound, caught
as it were in a loaded fire-passion
of persecution, an insane madness

of truth, compound philosophy that would
tire a marathon runner.
Everything in totality. Those who
are around have to beg for peace
for that captured soul must free itself – at least.

Pause

(*To be sung*:)

By the rivers of Babylon
Where we sat down
And there we wept
When we remembered Zion.

No man I know has called on
God's name so – with every statement
God's reference was the preference, in
happiness or in sadness same was the
name, private, public, always the same.
Plot entered plot, development created
broken straight lines carved into
luminous loneliness, love, loneliness,
lonesomeness, from Bristol to Nottingham,
to London he galloped. He ran with the
British Army in his head, the gloves,
the boots, the bed. He never wrote about
them but they were there! there! there!

So he ran from Silverburn House, all
around this neighbourhood, often like
a lonely cowboy, trying to dig deep
into the atrocities of this wet society,
sometimes misinterpreting, sometimes
misjudging but always trying –
you see he was searching for that self.
He wanted the people to know that
He cared; that he was worth something
not just a number and a name...
Watch the army brother! It can toy
with your brain, the war you

fight does not always belong to you
and the gun you carry could
back-fire too – remember, there're
no soldiers in St Paul's
He was a searcher, searching, searching man.

Pause Yeah.

Yeah, I argued with the police so fucking what!
So you scattered my bones among
the rose bushes... what's the
matter with you? I am not a baron!
Look, don't bother talk to me about
moral ethics, who good and what bad,
Jesus was a compassionate man,
so don't tell me, tell the people...
and stop telling them that I die from
heart attack. Tell the truth!
Stop being dishonest and lawless –
Tell dem the truth – yes!
This is death of a Blackman...

For the wicked dem carried
us away captivity, required
from us a song, how can we
sing King Alpha song in a strange land

T-Bone Wilson

WWW.OBERONBOOKS.COM

www.ingramcontent.com/pod-product-compliance
Ingram Content Group UK Ltd.
Pitfield, Milton Keynes, MK11 3LW, UK
UKHW020739280225
455688UK00013B/736

9 781840 021370